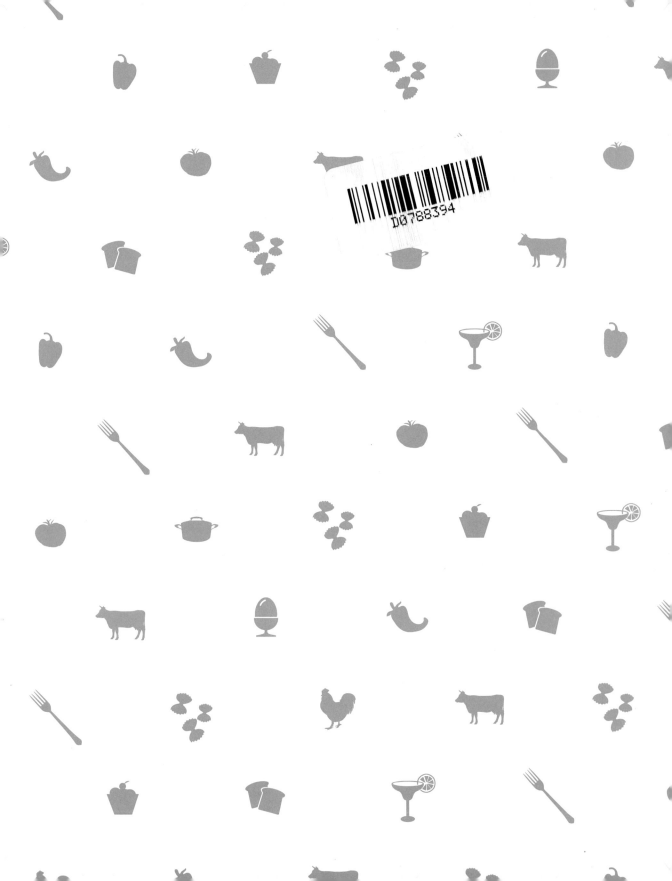

D0788394

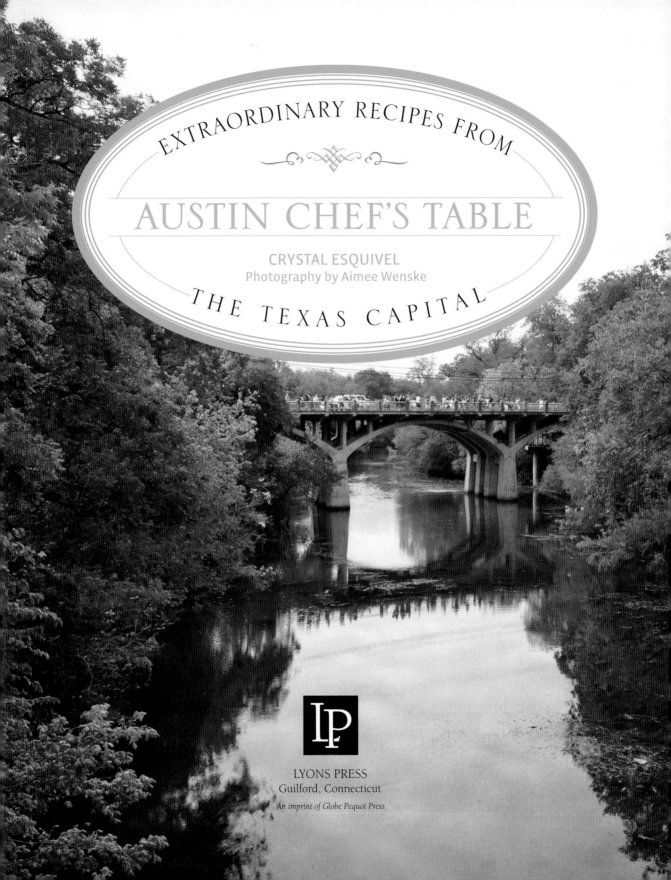

EXTRAORDINARY RECIPES FROM

AUSTIN CHEF'S TABLE

CRYSTAL ESQUIVEL
Photography by Aimee Wenske

THE TEXAS CAPITAL

LYONS PRESS
Guilford, Connecticut
An imprint of Globe Pequot Press

To buy books in quantity for corporate use
or incentives, call **(800) 962–0973**
or e-mail **premiums@GlobePequot.com.**

Lyons Press is an imprint of Globe Pequot Press.

All interior photos by Aimee Wenske unless otherwise noted.

Project Editor: David Legere
Text Design: Libby Kingsbury
Layout Artist: Nancy Freeborn

Library of Congress Cataloging-in-Publication Data is available on file.

ISBN 978-0-7627-8041-9

Printed in the United States of America

10 9 8 7 6 5 4 3 2 1

Restaurants and chefs often come and go, and menus are ever-changing.
We recommend you call ahead to obtain current information before
visiting any of the establishments in this book.

For Justin, my handsome prince

CONTENTS

Moscato d'Austin

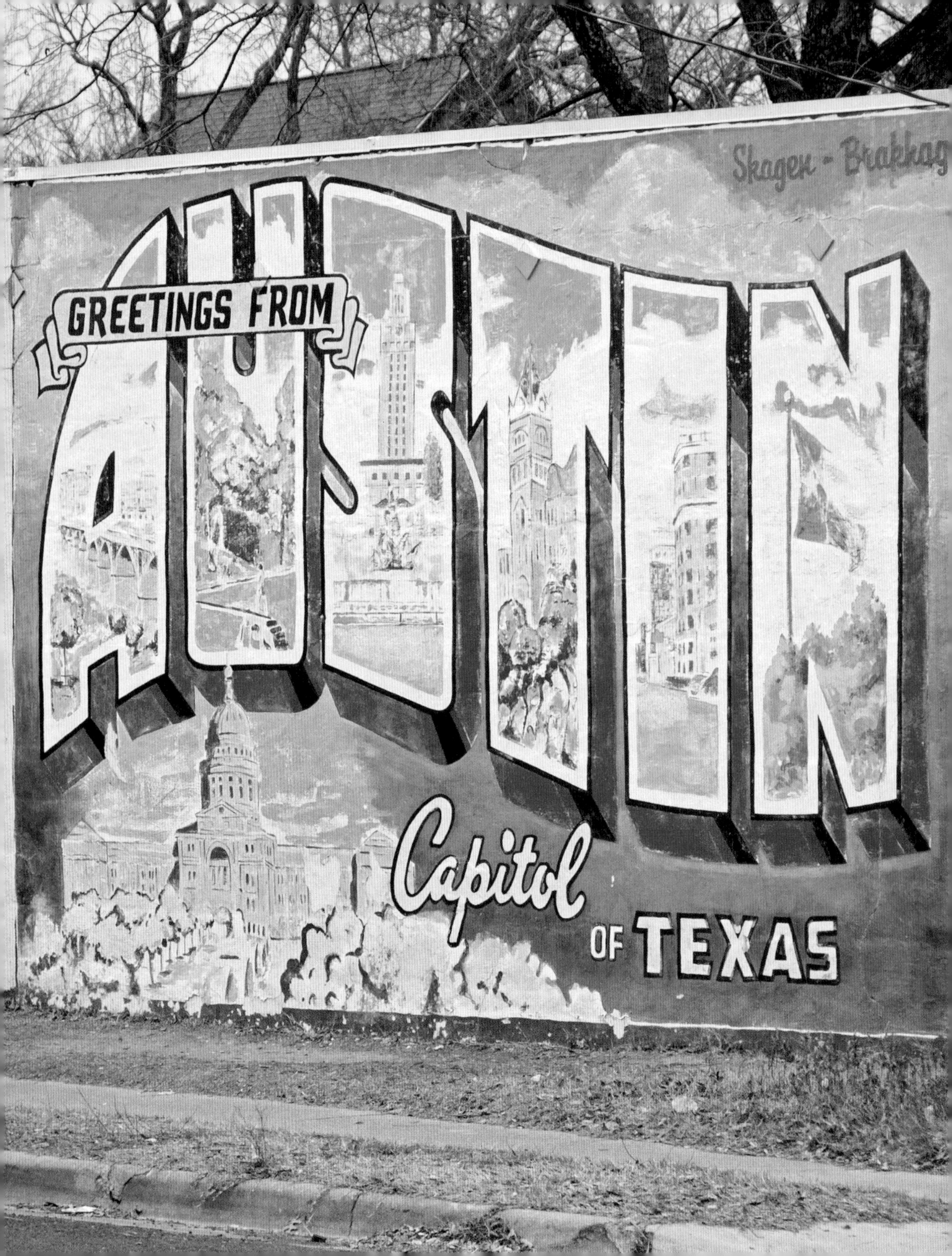
Skagen - Brakhag
GREETINGS FROM
AUSTIN
Capitol
OF TEXAS

Acknowledgments

I could not have finished this book without the support and encouragement from my husband, Justin. When I flopped on the bed and refused to write, he challenged me to brainstorm about my favorite restaurants. When I honestly believed I would never finish, he assured me that I was superwoman enough to do it. When I tested recipes and wasn't sure of the results, he provided honest feedback and offered to help. When I kept him up in the wee hours of the night talking about chefs and recipes and restaurants, he listened to my stories and laughed in all the right places. This book is for him.

To Aimee, my lovely photographer, who always had a smile and a sense of excitement with every photo shoot, every meeting, and every delay, thank you for coming along for the ride. I couldn't have wished for a better partner in crime.

To my editor, Katie Benoit Cardoso, thank you for your constant support, your prompt responses to questions, and your always encouraging words. You made this process so much easier than I thought it would be.

To my family, thank you for your encouragement, your enthusiasm, and your understanding as I buried myself in writing, writing, writing. Mom and Dad, you are the foundation that keeps me strong.

To my cheerleaders—Lindsay and Chad, Rachel and Logan, Erin and Nat, Natalie, Susan, Kim P., Bryan, Jodi, my supper club crew, my amazing blog readers, and the other bajillion people I'm forgetting—thank you SO much for your excitement and pride, your patience and support, and your willingness to hear me talk about restaurants EVERY time we spoke. Josh Pruett, thank you for your editing expertise. I love you all.

To all Austin's chefs, owners, managers, bartenders, and waitstaff who have become friends, confidants, and colleagues, thank you for sharing your creativity and expertise, for being patient with my unending questions, for countless conversations over coffee, and for inspiring me to write this book. You are the heart and soul of the *Austin Chef's Table*, and I am proud to present this book to you.

—Crystal

Thank you to my parents, who have always supported me and put my needs and aspirations before their own. Your sacrifices and love have made it possible for me to accomplish everything I have in life.

To Josh Pruett, for everything. It is because of your endless encouragement that I was able to create these photos and work on this project. I could not have done this without you.

To my friend Kathy Phan, who helped to kick off my career in food photography. Your sense of style and eye for design inspires me to always try a little harder and create something a little more fantastic.

To my best friend, Stephanie Vanelli, who recognized my love for photography early on and always encouraged me to follow this passion.

To Crystal, who has been so incredible to work with. Your organizational skills and spunk have made every meeting a delight. After this project, it is great to have come away with such an amazing friend.

To my friends, who provided focus, words of encouragement, and distractions when needed . . . I appreciate it all.

And to the city of Austin, I love you.

—Aimee

Introduction

There is so much to love about Austin. It is a young, vibrant community of creative individuals with a strong sense of local pride and Southern hospitality. As the capital of the state, the city is a great representation of the diverse cultures and political views of Texas. The climate is generally warm with mild winters, making it easy to enjoy the city's myriad green spaces, watering holes, and bike trails. The live music scene is vibrant, job growth has remained stronger than many other cities in the country, and Austin has been rated as one of the best cities to live and work in by several magazines. Most importantly for me, the food culture is fantastic.

In the past, Austin has mostly been known for its barbecue and breakfast tacos, and while those are still important parts of the local dining scene, in recent years the city has embraced a new generation of chefs and restaurants with exciting menus and design, and a focus on sustainability. The food truck scene just keeps growing, with entrepreneurs cooking up everything from crepes to *takoyaki,* and several of these trucks have moved on to become brick-and-mortar establishments. The talk of the town is now focused on which restaurants are opening, which chefs and bartenders are moving, and which ethnic restaurant is most authentic.

Tex-Mex cuisine is still an important part of the food scene, as it represents a true blend of Mexican and Southern culinary styles. Barbecue will always be a staple, as will chicken-fried steak. However, there has been a shift toward greener, healthier options, which are in high demand in a city as active and eco-aware as Austin. Restaurants are proud to use local ingredients as often as possible, to participate in recycling and composting programs, and to provide vegetarian, vegan, and gluten-free menus. Austinites have demanded a creative and sustainable food culture, and restaurants have been quick to provide just that.

When I moved to Austin ten years ago, I happily explored new restaurants and captured my experiences on my blog, *Poco-Cocoa (www.poco-cocoa.com).* I have seen the focus shift toward stylish decor and local ingredients, crafted cocktails, and menus inspired by the latest food trends. With every year, new restaurants take hold, and established restaurants elevate their techniques and menus. Needless to say, dining in Austin is a whole lot of fun.

Austin Chef's Table is a snapshot of our wonderful restaurant culture. Photographer Aimee Wenske and I were able to speak with local chefs and restaurateurs about their food philosophies and cooking styles, and many of them were thrilled to share their recipes and ideas. The result is this beautiful cookbook, full of fantastic recipes and stories from some of Austin's best eateries.

Divided by courses, the recipes in this book range from simple to complicated, and they come from a wide range of eateries—from delis to fine dining establishments. Many of the restaurants in this book were kind enough to share more than one recipe, which gives the reader a better sense of the type of food served at each place. Scattered throughout are cocktail recipes, as the cocktail culture in Austin is just as vibrant and important. Also included are a few sidebars that help to round out the picture of Austin's dining scene, as well as beautiful photographs of the finished dishes by Aimee Wenske.

I hope that this cookbook inspires you to try new recipes and restaurants, and to explore the creative and exciting food scene in Austin. Happy eating!

SOUPS, SALADS & SAUCES

Austin is said to have three seasons: spring, summer, and fall. Any amount of winter weather is generally fleeting and mild, but even so, locals take any opportunity to bundle up in sweaters and scarves, light fire pits, and enjoy warm and comforting soups. With long months of hot temperatures, the Austin climate is more suited for fresh, cool salads and lightly dressed grilled meats.

In the recipes that follow, chefs create complex, refined soups like the White Lobster Bisque with Tomato-Fresno Jam & Lobster Ricotta Fritter from Congress (page 15), while others simplify recipes to highlight the season's best produce, such as the Corn Soup from Fonda San Miguel (page 36) or the Roasted Red Pepper Soup from Andiamo (page 21). The fresh salads in this chapter are more than just a mix of lettuces—Second Bar + Kitchen's Endive & Apple Salad (page 4) is flavorful and refreshing (the green goddess dressing is stellar), and the cleverly named Once Upon a Time in Mexico Salad with Jalapeño-Lime Dressing from Alamo Drafthouse (page 30) is a meal in itself. Also included are a few sauces to dress up meals Austin-style, from the creamy Deluxe Tomatillo Sauce from Chuy's (page 34) to the light Achiote Marinade from Güero's Taco Bar (page 8).

Second Bar + Kitchen

200 Congress Avenue
Austin, TX 78701
(512) 827-2750
http://congressaustin.com/second/
Executive Chef: David Bull

Second Bar + Kitchen sits squarely among the hustle and bustle of Congress Avenue, under the Austonian, the city's tallest skyscraper. Its sleek, bright interior, excellent food, and creative cocktails draw in diners throughout the day and night.

An outdoor patio overlooks the busy 2nd Street District, while indoor tables and bar seats provide a lively venue for a meal or just drinks. The restaurant is open for lunch and dinner every day, with late hours on Friday and Saturday to accommodate the downtown crowds. Sunday brunch offers a leisurely pace and varied menu to round out the week.

Executive Chef David Bull has created a fun menu of snacks, small plates, pizzas, and entrees based on locally available ingredients. His "Natural American" cuisine is both exciting and approachable; guests can start with buffalo fried pickles and Gorgonzola or Chef Bull's family recipe for Pepperoni Soup, topped with mozzarella and served with garlic toast. The dinner menu features small plates of veal meatballs with fennel, garlic, and chive potato gnocchi as well as salt-and-pepper ahi with soy syrup, burned orange, and sprout salad. Pizzas are topped with short ribs and green chiles or black truffles and blue cheese, while the Congress Burger is dressed with shallot confit, gruyère, and horseradish pickles.

In addition to offering the full food menu, the bar serves craft beers, a large array of wines by the glass, and excellent cocktails made with top-notch spirits and fresh juices. The Gin + Jam features Citadelle gin and a dollop of house-made jam, while the Sweet Child O' Mine combines Flor de Caña rum, Cynar, lemon juice, and orgeat. After dinner, serious tipplers can wander over to Bar Congress, just one room away, for exquisite, spirit-heavy drinks and a more cozy, posh atmosphere.

Since it opened in 2010, Second Bar + Kitchen has become a cornerstone of the 2nd Street District, luring in guests of all ages and backgrounds with its creative menu made with the best local ingredients and its fresh and tasty cocktails. It's a delicious and spirited stop on any downtown jaunt.

PEPPERONI SOUP

This hearty, flavorful soup is a family recipe from Chef David Bull's grandmother. With the chunks of pepperoni, fresh herbs, and mozzarella topping, it tastes like a bite of a classic pepperoni pizza. Recipe courtesy of Executive Chef David Bull.

SERVES 4–6

2 tablespoons butter
3 tablespoons canola oil
2 cups diced pepperoni (about 7 ounces)
2 cups diced yellow onion
1 cup diced celery
1 tablespoon minced garlic
¼ teaspoon garlic powder
½ teaspoon garlic salt
¼ teaspoon celery seeds
⅛ teaspoon red chile flakes
2 tablespoons chopped fresh basil
1 tablespoon chopped fresh oregano
1½ tablespoons chopped fresh parsley
1 cup tomato puree
¼ cup Sauternes or other sweet white wine
2 cups tomato juice
1 cup tomato sauce
1 cup water
Salt and pepper to taste
1 cup shredded mozzarella cheese
Toasted garlic bread, for dipping

Add the butter and oil to a large soup pot over medium heat, and heat until butter is melted.

Add pepperoni and cook about 6–8 minutes, stirring occasionally, until the fat is rendered. Add onion, celery, garlic, garlic powder, garlic salt, celery seeds, red chile flakes, basil, oregano, and parsley. Cook for about 10–12 minutes, stirring occasionally, until the vegetables are tender but not browned.

Add the tomato puree; stir to mix well. Cook for a few minutes to toast the puree slightly.

Add the wine and deglaze the pot. Cook until liquid is reduced by half and the soup thickens, about 4–6 minutes.

Add tomato juice, tomato sauce, and water and bring to a boil; reduce heat to low and simmer for 20 minutes. Season to taste with salt and pepper.

Serve topped with mozzarella cheese and with toasted garlic bread for dipping.

Endive & Apple Salad

The addition of grapes, walnuts, and apple to this endive salad makes it reminiscent of a Waldorf salad, but the creamy and bright green goddess dressing takes it over the top. Recipe courtesy of Executive Chef David Bull.

SERVES 4

For green goddess dressing:

½ cup buttermilk
½ cup mayonnaise
¼ cup crumbled goat cheese
1 tablespoon chopped fresh basil
1 tablespoon chopped fresh tarragon leaves
2 tablespoons chopped fresh Italian parsley
2 tablespoons apple cider vinegar
Salt and pepper to taste

For the salad:

4 heads endive, leaves separated
1 cup green grapes, cut in half lengthwise
1 Granny Smith apple, cored and julienned
¼ cup walnuts, toasted and chopped
¼ cup sunflower sprouts
½ cup crumbled goat cheese

To prepare the dressing: Place all ingredients in a blender and puree at lowest setting. When the ingredients begin to combine, increase to high speed and blend until the herbs are completely pulverized. Season with salt and pepper to taste; chill until ready to use.

To prepare the salad: Combine the endive, grapes, apple, and 1 cup chilled dressing in a large bowl. Toss until everything is nicely coated with the dressing. Divide the endive mixture among four chilled plates. For each plate, sprinkle walnuts, sprouts, and goat cheese over the endive mixture. Drizzle remaining dressing around the plates.

Perfect Pairing

SWEET CHILD O' MINE

Second Bar + Kitchen serves up inventive cocktails that are still approachable to the average diner. This drink mixes the sweetness of orgeat and rum with a hint of bitterness from the Cynar for a balanced, easy-to-sip treat. Recipe courtesy of Barman Darren Makowsky.

SERVES 1

1½ ounces Flor de Caña rum
½ ounce Cynar
½ ounce freshly squeezed lemon juice
½ ounce orgeat
Ice
Orange peel, for garnish

Combine the first four ingredients in a shaker with ice. Shake until chilled, then strain into a chilled coupe glass. Garnish with twisted orange peel.

GÜERO'S TACO BAR

1412 SOUTH CONGRESS AVENUE
AUSTIN, TX 78704
(512) 447-7688
WWW.GUEROSTACOBAR.COM
OWNERS: ROB AND CATHY LIPPINCOTT

Since 1986, Güero's Taco Bar has been serving food from interior Mexico with a splash of Tex-Mex. In 1995, the owners, Rob and Cathy Lippincott, renovated an old feed store built in the 1800s, and the current Güero's location was born. With its prime spot on busy South Congress Avenue, a large outdoor beer garden, fresh margaritas, and handmade tortillas, Güero's remains a favorite destination for tourists and locals alike.

A few sidewalk tables provide the ultimate people-watching spot, as crowds walk through the area on their way to vintage shops, art galleries, and live music venues. Tables inside are often dotted with visiting celebrities, especially during any of Austin's great events such as South by Southwest, the Austin City Limits Music Festival, or the Austin Film Festival. While every diner has his or her preferred dishes, the tacos, served on fresh, handmade corn tortillas, are crowd favorites. Marinated pork comes topped with onions, cilantro, and pineapple, while the popular grilled fish tacos are smothered in creamy tequila aioli. Enchiladas, chiles rellenos, and *caldo de pollo* are also good choices, and all of the menu items are even better washed down with one of Güero's house margaritas. Made simply with tequila, Cointreau, and key lime juice, the drinks are fresh, tart, and surprisingly low in calories.

The outdoor beer garden features live music several nights a week under a giant oak tree strung with lights, and the space fills up on weekends with South Congress shoppers and diners. A lively meal with friends, a quick taco and margarita at the bar, or a cold beer in the Oak Garden are all excellent ways to experience the laid-back atmosphere and South Congress vibe of Güero's.

Achiote Marinade

Güero's ever-popular chicken tacos al carbon feature a smoky and fresh achiote chicken marinade. The most important ingredient in the marinade is achiote paste, made from annatto seeds and popular in the cooking of the Oaxaca and Yucatán regions of Mexico. The paste can be found in specialty and Mexican markets. Recipe courtesy of Cathy Lippincott.

MAKES 2½ CUPS MARINADE

1 cup white vinegar
1½ (3.5-ounce) bars achiote paste
1 cup orange juice

Whisk ingredients together. Use as a marinade for your choice of meat: Try grilled chicken or pork, which can then be made into tacos on corn or flour tortillas.

TEQUILA AIOLI

The grilled fish tacos at Güero's are topped with a dollop of creamy tequila aioli, a perfect spicy accompaniment to the fresh corn tortillas and grilled fish. The sauce gets a bit of heat from the adobo sauce (easily spooned from a can of chipotle chiles) and a nice depth from the addition of your favorite tequila. Recipe courtesy of Cathy Lippincott.

MAKES 3 CUPS

2 cups mayonnaise
½ cup adobo sauce from canned chipotle chiles
½ teaspoon chopped fresh oregano
6 tablespoons tequila
½ cup freshly squeezed orange juice

Whisk all ingredients together. Use as a topping for grilled fish, or try grilled tilapia served in corn tortillas, topped with shredded white cabbage and a dollop of the tequila aioli.

Perfect Pairing

GÜERO'S FAMOUS MARGARITA

Güero's owner Cathy Lippincott is proud of their margaritas, which have always been prepared with fresh ingredients and without any sweeteners. At the restaurant, guests have a choice of tequilas, shaken with freshly squeezed key lime juice and Cointreau. Recipe courtesy of Cathy Lippincott.

SERVES 1

1¼ ounces tequila
¾ ounce triple sec, Cointreau, or Grand Marnier
¾ ounce freshly squeezed key lime juice
Ice

Combine all ingredients in a shaker and shake vigorously, until bits of ice have broken up in the mixture. Strain and pour either up or on the rocks.

EASTSIDE CAFE

2113 MANOR ROAD
AUSTIN, TX 78722
(512) 476-5858
WWW.EASTSIDECAFEAUSTIN.COM
OWNER/EXECUTIVE CHEF: ELAINE MARTIN

Elaine Martin opened Eastside Cafe in 1988 with the goal of making good, fresh food that was also accessible and reasonably priced. Over the years, the cafe has become one of Austin's favorite eateries, known for its garden-fresh vegetables, seasonal menus, and well-executed home-style food.

Chef Martin was first inspired by her mother and grandmother, who were excellent home cooks. She now looks for new dish ideas in books, on her travels, and from culinary icons such as Alice Waters, whose farm-to-table approach is closely in line with her own. Creating exciting and flavorful dishes using produce that is seasonally and locally available is a challenge that Chef Martin embraces wholeheartedly.

The cafe's garden produces some of the vegetables that are featured on the menu, and the happy chickens on-site supply some of the eggs. The restaurant also sources additional eggs, vegetables, and fruits from local farms. This garden-to-table approach results in creative seasonal dishes—one summer's bumper crop of cucumbers inspired

Chef Martin to preserve them by making pickles, which have now become a favorite item on the menu. The seasonal side dishes and soups at Eastside Cafe are legendary, from the acorn squash with soy-ginger sauce to the strawberry soup.

The restaurant is always busy, whether with business lunches, leisurely brunches, or romantic dinners. The original house is made up of several cozy dining rooms, and the additional garden room in back provides an airy space with windows overlooking the vegetables growing nearby.

Chef Martin is proud of the respectful and service-oriented environment she has cultivated with her staff, many of whom have been employed at the restaurant for ten to fifteen years. Together, they have succeeded in making Eastside Cafe a charming restaurant with honest and approachable fresh food.

Spicy Tomato Soup

Chef Martin's Spicy Tomato Soup is on regular rotation on the menu. The soup has bright flavors and a velvety smoothness, and the soup base itself is vegan. At the restaurant, the soup is topped with fried tortilla strips and grated Monterey Jack cheese, which can easily be omitted for a truly vegan dish. Pair this with an ice-cold beer for a comforting autumn lunch. Recipe courtesy of Executive Chef Elaine Martin.

SERVES 8–10

2 tablespoons olive oil

2 cups diced onions

2 corn tortillas, torn into pieces

1 (10-ounce) can diced tomatoes with green chiles

1 teaspoon minced, seeded fresh jalapeño

1 teaspoon minced garlic

¼ teaspoon ground cumin

2 (14½-ounce) cans whole tomatoes

8 cups vegetable stock

1 teaspoon salt

¼ teaspoon black pepper

Fried tortilla strips, for garnish

½ cup grated Monterey Jack cheese, for garnish

Heat olive oil in a large soup pot over medium heat. Sauté the onions and corn tortillas over low heat for 15 minutes, or until browned. Add tomatoes with chiles, jalapeños, garlic, cumin, whole tomatoes, and vegetable stock. Bring to a boil; reduce heat and simmer for 30 minutes. Remove from heat and cool slightly.

Transfer tomato mixture to a blender or food processor and puree until smooth. Return puree to soup pot and season with salt and pepper. Serve garnished with fried tortilla strips and grated cheese.

Salsa

Eastside Cafe's salsa is made from a simple recipe and readily available ingredients. Chef Martin recommends tossing in any of your favorite additions—try adding more jalapeños or a couple of chipotle chiles for a spicier, smoky version. At the restaurant, this vegan salsa is served as an appetizer with tortilla chips, as well as in the popular huevos Mexicanos on the brunch menu. Recipe courtesy of Executive Chef Elaine Martin.

MAKES 4 CUPS

1 cup diced onions

1 tablespoon minced canned jalapeños

½ cup minced fresh cilantro

1 teaspoon minced fresh garlic

1 (10-ounce can) diced tomatoes with green chiles

1 (14½-ounce) can diced tomatoes

½ cup diced green bell pepper

½ teaspoon salt

1½ teaspoons fresh lime juice

Combine all ingredients in a bowl. Puree in a food processor (you may have to do this in batches) until it reaches desired consistency.

Congress

200 Congress Avenue
Austin, TX 78701
(512) 827-2760
http://congressaustin.com/congress/
Executive Chef: David Bull

Located at the base of the beautiful Austonian skyscraper, Congress is by far one of Austin's most luxurious and celebrated dining experiences. Executive Chef David Bull, who is also the Executive Chef of Second Bar + Kitchen, crafts each day's dinner menu based on ingredients that are locally and seasonally available.

Chef Bull offers a three-course and a seven-course menu daily. The three-course menu allows diners to choose dishes from a list of options, mixing and matching to meet their mood for the evening. Guests might start with a Bosc pear and endive salad with *burrata* and roasted cauliflower, then move on to white lobster bisque or carrot ravioli with lemongrass and shiso.

The seven-course tasting menu is personally selected by the chef and takes diners through a paced evening of incredible dishes. A beverage pairing is available as well, which features expertly paired wines, beers, and cocktails for each course. Delicate desserts such as caramel pudding with cocoa "soil" and chocolate beignets with roasted-banana ice cream provide a decadent and exquisite ending to the meal.

The dining room is elegant and refined, with plush white seats and rich wood accents. Service is impeccable from the moment you are greeted at the door, and the entire experience is somehow quiet but exciting. With each course, diners can expect the highest quality of ingredients, preparation, and service.

Since its opening in 2010, Congress has garnered quite a few awards and accolades, including the title of *Texas Monthly*'s "Best New Restaurant" in Texas in 2012, as well as June Rodil's selection as one of the "Best New Sommeliers of 2011" by *Wine & Spirits* magazine. The restaurant continues to be a shining star of culinary excellence in Austin.

White Lobster Bisque with Fresno-Tomato Jam & Lobster Ricotta Fritter

This exquisite dish starts with a rich base of lobster stock, which is transformed into a creamy and decadent bisque. The bright and spicy Fresno chile and tomato jam provides an acidic balance, while the lobster fritter adds crunch and texture. Recipe courtesy of Executive Chef David Bull.

SERVES 4

For the white lobster bisque:

2 tablespoons canola oil
1 small yellow onion, chopped
2 celery stalks, chopped
½ cup chopped fennel
1 shallot, chopped
3 garlic cloves, chopped
1½ teaspoons black peppercorns
1½ teaspoons fennel seed
2 bay leaves
½ cup brandy
½ cup sherry
1 cup white wine
2 cups lobster or chicken stock
5 lobster heads
4 cups heavy cream
¼ cup cornstarch
½ cup water

For the Fresno-tomato jam:

1 cup diced and drained canned tomatoes,
    with 1 cup tomato juice reserved
1 tablespoon unsalted butter
½ cup minced shallots
¼ cup diced, seeded Fresno chiles
½ cup sugar
½ cup red wine vinegar
1 teaspoon salt

For the lobster ricotta fritters:

½ cup all-purpose flour
1 teaspoon baking powder
1 teaspoon fine sea salt
1½ teaspoons finely chopped fresh parsley
½ cup cornmeal
2 tablespoons whole milk ricotta cheese
½ cup whole milk
1 tablespoon maple syrup
½ cup diced cooked lobster meat
Oil, for frying
Salt to taste
Micro celery leaves, for garnish

Special equipment:

Outdoor or stove-top smoker and mesquite wood chips
Small, quarter-size ice cream scoop
2-inch ring molds

To prepare the white lobster bisque: Heat the canola oil in a large soup pot over low heat. Add the onion, celery, fennel, shallot, and garlic; sweat for 10–15 minutes, being careful not to brown or color any of the vegetables.

Add the peppercorns, fennel seed, and bay leaf; cook for 2–3 minutes.

Deglaze the pot with brandy, sherry, and white wine. Bring the mixture to a boil over high heat.

Add the lobster or chicken stock and lobster heads; simmer and reduce liquid by half.

Add the heavy cream and bring mixture to a boil once again.

In a small bowl, combine the cornstarch and water. Whisk the cornstarch slurry into the boiling mixture. Turn heat to low and cook for 20 minutes at a low simmer.

To prepare the Fresno-tomato jam: Smoke the diced tomatoes using an outdoor smoker or stove-top smoker for 30–35 minutes at 155°F or until the tomatoes have taken on a smoky flavor.

Add the butter to a large saucepan over medium heat. Add the shallots and chiles and sweat for 3–4 minutes.

Add the sugar, red wine vinegar, and reserved tomato juice; bring to a boil. Reduce heat to low and simmer for 15 minutes, or until a syrupy consistency is reached.

Remove the mixture from the heat and fold in the smoked tomatoes and salt. Allow the mixture to cool to room temperature.

To prepare the lobster ricotta fritters: Combine the flour, baking powder, salt, parsley, and cornmeal.

In a separate bowl, combine the ricotta, whole milk, and maple syrup.

Add the wet mixture to the dry mixture and stir to incorporate. Fold in the cooked lobster meat. Allow mixture to rest at room temperature for 30 minutes.

Heat 2 inches oil to 350°F in a cast-iron skillet or a deep fryer.

Using a small ice-cream scoop, drop the fritter batter carefully into the hot oil. Fry the fritters for 2–3 minutes on all sides, or until golden brown and crisp.

Remove fritters from oil, drain on paper towels, and immediately season with salt. Keep warm until ready for assembly.

To serve: Scoop the Fresno-tomato jam into a 2-inch ring mold in the center of each soup bowl; remove the ring. Top the jam with a fritter and garnish the base of the bowl with micro celery leaves. Using a small creamer, pitcher, or beaker, pour the hot bisque into each bowl at the table.

Perfect Pairing

Recipe courtesy of Bar Manager Jason Stevens

THE ORACLE
SERVES 1

For the smoked orange bitters:

2 ounces Regans #6 orange bitters
1 ounce Angostura orange bitters
1 teaspoon loose Lapsang Souchong tea

For the cocktail:

1¾ ounces Sazerac 6-Year Rye
¾ ounce Cocchi Vermouth di Torino
½ ounce Averna Amaro
1 generous bar spoon Del Maguey
    Chichicapa Mezcal
Ice
1 Luxardo maraschino cherry

To prepare the smoked orange bitters:
Combine all ingredients in a sealable glass jar. Infuse for 10 minutes, shaking several times. Strain out the tea using a fine-mesh strainer. Pour mixture into a small dropper bottle.

To prepare the cocktail: Combine rye, vermouth, amaro, and mezcal in a mixing glass with ice. Stir until chilled, then strain into a chilled coupe glass. Garnish with a cherry and 5 drops of the smoked orange bitters on the top for aroma.

PATIO DINING

Austin's warm weather means that for most of the year, dining alfresco is a great option. Restaurants have taken advantage of this throughout the city, maximizing seating and creating welcoming outdoor waiting areas. The patio has become an important, almost expected addition to any new restaurant that opens.

Restaurant patios are usually equipped with fans and/or misters to keep diners comfortable during Austin's summer heat. Moderate winter temperatures are kept at bay with fire pits and outdoor heaters. The patio is often the preferred seating area throughout the year.

Many downtown bars have casual patios equipped with full bars and televisions, while even upscale restaurants like FINO (page 46) and Paggi House (page 102) pride themselves on beautiful outdoor seating and decor. Olive & June (www.oliveandjune-austin.com) and Perla's (www.perlasaustin.com) boast huge patios that offer just as much seating as the indoor areas, while Contigo (page 57) and Cuatros (www.cuatrosaustin.com) are almost entirely outdoors. On Lake Austin, the Hula Hut (www.hulahut.com), Mozart's (www.mozartscoffee.com), and Abel's on the Lake (www.abelsonthelake.com) feature large outdoor seating areas hovering over the lake.

Seared Sea Scallop with Jícama Salad, Coconut Cream, Cocoa Nibs & Chocolate Mint

This elegant dish pairs lightly seared sea scallops with a fresh and crispy jícama salad. The coconut cream and cocoa nib crumble add an earthy and creamy accent to the dish. Recipe courtesy of Executive Chef David Bull.

SERVES 4

For the cocoa nib crumble:

¾ cup sugar

2 tablespoons light corn syrup

¼ cup water

2 tablespoons unsalted butter

½ teaspoon baking soda

¼ cup cocoa nibs (partially ground cacao beans, available at specialty grocery stores)

2–4 tablespoons tapioca starch

For the lime vinaigrette:

¼ cup lime juice

2 tablespoons extra-virgin olive oil

Sea salt to taste

For the jicama-mint salad:

¼ cup shredded fresh coconut, toasted

¼ cup fresh mint, julienned

4 cups julienned jícama

Sea salt to taste

For the coconut cream:

1 cup heavy cream

½ cup cream of coconut (such as Coco Lopez)

For the seared sea scallops:

2 tablespoons canola oil

4 large (U/10) sea scallops

Sea salt to taste

Maldon sea salt to taste

4 chocolate mint leaves (a variety of mint with a subtle chocolate flavor), for garnish

Special equipment:

2 nonstick silicone baking mats to fit a baking sheet

To prepare the cocoa nib crumble: Combine the sugar, corn syrup, water, and butter in a small saucepan over medium heat. Bring the liquid to a simmer and cook for 12–15 minutes, or until it reaches a light caramel color. Remove from the heat.

In a separate bowl, combine the baking soda and cocoa nibs.

Add the cocoa nib mixture to the caramel and return to heat; cook until a rich amber color is reached.

While the mixture is still hot, pour onto a baking sheet lined with a silicone baking mat; spread out as thinly as possible. Place another silicone liner on top of the mixture. Using a rolling pin, roll the mixture out into a thin, even layer. Allow the mixture to cool to room temperature.

Once completely cooled, break the mixture into pieces; place in a food processor. Add 2 tablespoons of tapioca starch and pulse until a coarse sand consistency is reached. Add more tapioca starch as needed to reach the proper consistency. Reserve the crumble in an airtight container until ready for assembly.

To prepare the lime vinaigrette: Whisk together the lime juice and olive oil until well combined. Season with salt to taste.

To prepare the jicama-mint salad: Mix the toasted coconut with the mint and jícama. Toss with the lime vinaigrette and season with salt to taste.

To prepare the coconut cream: Combine the heavy cream and cream of coconut in a large mixing bowl. Whisk or beat thoroughly until soft peaks are formed.

To prepare the seared sea scallops: Heat the canola oil in a large sauté pan over high heat. Season the scallops on all sides with sea salt.

Allow the oil to begin to smoke; add scallops and sear on each side for 2–3 minutes, creating a dark brown crust on the top and bottom of each. Remove the scallops from the pan and allow to rest 5 minutes before plating.

To serve: Slice the scallops into three even pieces from top to bottom to form square-shaped slices. Lay the scallop slices in a straight line on each plate, leaving 1-inch gaps between each slice.

Place small dollops of the coconut cream in between each scallop; place jícama-mint salad directly on top of the coconut cream. Sprinkle the cocoa nib crumble in a straight line over the scallops.

Season the scallops with sea salt to taste and garnish each slice with a small leaf of chocolate mint.

Andiamo Ristorante

2521 Rutland Drive
Austin, TX 78758
(512) 719-3377
http://andiamoitaliano.com/
Owner: Daniela Marcone

Tucked into a strip mall in north Austin, Andiamo is a surprisingly elegant restaurant serving fine Italian food. Italian owner Daniela Marcone showcases her passion for her country and its food with each meal the restaurant serves.

Once inside, guests will find a refined, intimate space with gorgeous paintings of Italian hillsides and alleyways. Tables are beautifully set, and the atmosphere is both classy and comfortable. Waitstaff are welcoming, professional, and happy to guide diners through the menu and suggest pairings from the all-Italian wine list.

Marcone insists on authenticity in the recipes and preparation of the dishes. Everything is made from scratch, from breads to pastas, and much of the produce is sourced from local farmers' markets. Specialty meats and cheeses are imported from Italy, and wines are carefully chosen based on Marcone's relationships with the vintners. Diners won't find pizza or meatballs on the menu—the focus is on cooking the freshest ingredients in the Italian style.

Each evening, a five-course chef's tasting menu is available, as well as a vegetarian version. Alternatively, diners can choose from antipasti, soups, salads, pastas, and entrees. Small plates range from mussels with farro and spicy white wine sauce to seared scallops with capers and brandy cream. Pasta dishes include house-made ravioli filled with ricotta and mushrooms, and penne tossed with shrimp, roasted red peppers, and asparagus. Entrees like traditional veal scaloppine and crab-stuffed rainbow trout are just as tempting, and the desserts—such as Nutella and chocolate tart, tiramisu, and zabaglione—are not to be missed.

Each month, Andiamo hosts a wine dinner featuring a sommelier's pairings of Italian wines and special dinner items. The restaurant also serves weekday lunch, which is a great time to stop in and try a few dishes. This little gem of a restaurant, with its excellent food and service, is worth the short drive north.

FENNEL SALAD WITH WALNUTS & TRUFFLE OIL

This elegant salad is simply dressed with lemon juice and truffle oil, allowing the delicate flavors of the fennel, creamy goat cheese, and walnuts to shine. Recipe courtesy of Executive Chef José Lópes.

SERVES 1

1 cup shaved or very thinly sliced fennel
½ teaspoon fresh lemon juice
½ teaspoon truffle oil
Salt to taste
1 tablespoon walnuts
1 tablespoon crumbled goat cheese

In a large bowl, toss the fennel with the lemon juice and truffle oil, adding salt to taste. Sprinkle walnuts and goat cheese over the salad.

ROASTED RED PEPPER SOUP

This smooth and creamy soup gets its texture from potatoes and its bright flavor from the roasted red peppers. At Andiamo, the soup is topped with a few croutons and a drizzle of extra-virgin olive oil. Recipe courtesy of Executive Chef José Lópes.

SERVES 8

6 tablespoons (¾ stick) unsalted butter
½ medium yellow onion, chopped
2 large red bell peppers, roasted, peeled, seeded, and diced
2 small russet potatoes (about 1 pound), diced
6 cups vegetable stock
Salt to taste

Melt the butter in a large soup pot over medium heat. Add the onions and cook, stirring, just until translucent. Add the roasted peppers and potatoes and sauté together for about 5 minutes.

Add the vegetable stock and simmer for about 15 minutes, or until the potatoes are tender. Add salt to taste.

Transfer the soup to a blender and carefully puree until smooth (you may need to do this in small batches with the lid slightly askew to allow steam to escape). Adjust seasoning, if needed, and serve hot.

Justine's Brasserie

4710 East 5th Street
Austin, TX 78702
(512) 385-2900
http://justines1937.com/
Owners: Justine Gilcrease and Pierre Pelegrin

At the end of a dark, industrial street in east Austin lies a tiny, twinkle-lit oasis. Justine's is a renovated 1937 bungalow that was transformed into an homage to the classic French brasserie. Owners Justine Gilcrease and Pierre Pelegrin opened the cozy and intimate restaurant in 2009, with the goal of creating a lively spot where diners are welcomed well into the evening and offered a full menu of solid French fare. Outside, tiny bistro tables and folding chairs sit under a white canopy, with strings of white lights creating a romantic and laid-back ambience. A *pétanque* court keeps visitors busy while they wait for their tables.

Inside, Justine's is full of dark and sexy corners, enclosed in red-and-black walls and outfitted with small marble tables and dark wooden chairs. The bar is small and welcoming, with bartenders serving from a fun and varied cocktail and wine list. Shelves of vinyl records provide vintage jazz tunes with that unmistakable scratchy turntable sound.

Once guests have been seated, they can choose from several aperitifs, including kir royale and pastis. A short but varied wine list offers well-priced options, while the full bar can whip up any number of new and classic cocktails. Chalkboards around the restaurant list the day's wine and food specials.

Justine's food menu is a basic course in classic French dishes, all of them expertly prepared. Small plates of escargot come drenched in garlicky butter, while the whole artichoke comes simply cooked with lemon butter for dipping. The charcuterie plate features rillettes and pâtés prepared in-house, and the onion soup is a rich, flavorful rendition smothered in melted gruyère.

Entrees include a perfectly cooked pork chop served with creamy potato gratin; a juicy, flavorful steak served with crispy frites and topped with pastis-infused herb butter, Roquefort, or sauce au poivre; and flavorful ratatouille. The crème brûlée and chocolate-pear tart are simple but delicious, and there are often dessert specials featuring seasonal fruits.

Justine's location in far east Austin makes it a perfect stop for late-night arrivals from the airport, and its blinking neon sign is a beacon for late-night diners ready to spend a few hours enjoying great food, drinks, and company. Visiting Justine's is like being dropped into a dreamy, European corner of the world, where the night reigns and the laughter spills freely.

Montpellier Butter

This tart and flavorful butter sauce is excellent served with fish, boiled potatoes, cooked vegetables, seared steak, or just spread over crusty bread. At Justine's it is served with broiled Atlantic cod and a tomato, leek, and spinach fondue. Recipe courtesy of Executive Chef Casey Wilcox.

MAKES ABOUT 2½ CUPS

½ cup parsley leaves

½ cup watercress

¼ cup tarragon leaves

½ cup spinach

¼ cup sliced shallots

1½ cloves garlic

¾ cup canola oil, olive oil, or a blend

2 egg yolks

1½ anchovies

3 cornichons

1 tablespoon capers

Juice of ½ lemon

¼ teaspoon white vinegar

¼ teaspoon cayenne pepper

¼ teaspoon ground black pepper

1 teaspoon salt

1¼ cups (2½ sticks) softened, unsalted butter

Bring a large pot of water to a boil over high heat. Prepare an ice bath by filling a large bowl with ice water.

When the pot of water comes to a boil, add the parsley, watercress, tarragon, spinach, shallots, and garlic. Blanch for 1–2 minutes, until the greens brighten. Scoop the ingredients from the pot and immediately shock them in the ice bath. Drain and pat the ingredients dry.

Put the drained herb mixture in a blender and puree until well chopped. Slowly add the oil in a steady stream while the blender is running to create an emulsion. Set aside.

In a food processor, combine egg yolks, anchovies, cornichons, capers, lemon juice, vinegar, cayenne, black pepper, and salt. Process for 2 minutes, until smooth. Slowly add half of the herb-oil mixture in a steady stream while the processor is running. Add butter in small amounts, pureeing constantly. Finally, add the remaining herb-oil mixture in a steady stream while processing to emulsify. The butter will keep for 1–2 days (the herbs will darken after that, but the butter will still be good for up to a week).

PIPERADE

A smooth emulsion of oil and roasted red peppers, Justine's piperade is served with seared scallops, fingerling potatoes, and chorizo. It is a versatile Basque-influenced sauce that can also be served with fish, grilled asparagus, roasted squash, chicken, or strongly flavored small fish such as sardines or mackerel. Recipe courtesy of Executive Chef Casey Wilcox.

MAKES ABOUT 1 CUP

½ cup olive oil

1 cup sliced shallots

1 cup sliced red bell peppers

8 cloves garlic, thinly sliced

6 cherry tomatoes, halved

1 teaspoon salt

1 teaspoon Espelette chile pepper (*piment d'Espelette*), available in specialty grocery stores; hot paprika can be substituted

½ teaspoon ground black pepper

3 tablespoons white wine

3 tablespoons water

10 flat-leaf parsley leaves

1 ounce Spanish chorizo, thinly sliced

In a medium saucepan, combine olive oil, shallots, bell peppers, garlic, tomatoes, salt, Espelette pepper, and black pepper. Bring heat up to medium and sauté until the vegetables start to break down and begin to brown.

Add wine and water, and stir continuously as the liquid reduces. The oil will emulsify and thicken slightly. If the emulsification breaks, add 1 teaspoon hot water and stir vigorously to re-emulsify.

Finish the sauce with parsley leaves and chorizo and cook for just a minute to heat through. Serve immediately.

Perfect Pairing

L'ENFANT TERRIBLE

SERVES 1

This bright and slightly sweet cocktail is popular at Justine's, both as a predinner drink and an accompaniment to lighter first courses. Recipe courtesy of Justine's.

2 ounces citrus vodka (like Ketel One Citroen)

1½ ounces St-Germain elderflower liqueur

1 ounce lime juice

Splash of cranberry juice

Splash of simple syrup

Ice

Lime slice, for garnish

Combine all ingredients except lime slice in a cocktail shaker and shake well. Strain into a chilled martini glass and garnish with lime slice.

To prepare simple syrup: Place 1 cup granulated sugar and 1 cup water in a saucepan. Over medium heat, stir until dissolved. Cool, and pour into a very clean bottle. Refrigerated, simple syrup keeps indefinitely.

MULBERRY

360 NUECES STREET, SUITE 20
AUSTIN, TX 78701
(512) 320-0297
HTTP://MULBERRYAUSTIN.COM/
OWNER: MICHAEL POLOMBO; EXECUTIVE CHEF: JACOB WEAVER

Tucked away at the bottom of the 360 Tower in downtown Austin, Mulberry is a minuscule wine bar serving contemporary American food. Owned by Michael Polombo, this restaurant was inspired by his tiny Bin 71 restaurant in New York City.

Mulberry has a couple of tables inside, plus seats at the beautiful U-shaped bar. The outside patio offers a few more tables. The atmosphere is cozy and inviting, and locals stop in throughout the evening for snacks and drinks.

The menu features updated American classics as well as dishes inspired by the different cultures that contribute to the American identity. Executive Chef Jacob Weaver prefers to focus on just a few great flavors for each dish, keeping it simple but elevated while highlighting the best ingredients available.

Small plates include the popular devils on horseback—sweet dates stuffed with Gorgonzola and wrapped in bacon—as well as house-made ricotta crostini and flavorful meatballs in a white wine and lemon broth. Along with salads, soups, and sandwiches, the entrees feature local produce and some local proteins. Coffee-rubbed lamb saddle is served with polenta, yogurt, and spicy celery salad, while the house-made pasta is tossed with sun-dried tomatoes, ricotta, and olives. Mulberry also serves brunch on the weekends, with truffled frittatas, blueberry pancakes, and brioche french toast.

The list of over 150 wines is carefully selected by sommelier Brian Phillips and includes a large selection of wines by the glass. Phillips has even created his own wine, named Ground Up, which is served at the restaurant.

On any given evening, thanks to Austin's balmy climate, Mulberry's patio is full of guests sipping drinks and chatting,

enjoying the great service and urban feel. With its location off the main streets, it feels hidden, a place with many local regulars who know they can always find a friendly smile and great glass of wine.

Brussels Sprout Salad

This salad quickly became a favorite of Mulberry's diners. Frying the brussels sprouts results in a caramelized flavor and texture, while tossing them with the fresh leaves and radishes keeps the dish from being too heavy. Recipe courtesy of Executive Chef Jacob Weaver.

SERVES 4

For the goat cheese-ranch dressing:

2 egg yolks

Approximately 3 tablespoons buttermilk

1 cup canola oil

1 bunch green onions, green tops only, roughly chopped

4 ounces chèvre

Salt to taste

1 tablespoon chopped parsley

1 tablespoon coarsely cracked black pepper

For the salad:

Vegetable or peanut oil, for frying

1 pound brussels sprouts, woody ends trimmed off, quartered

Juice of 1 lemon, or more to taste

Salt to taste

3–4 radishes, very thinly sliced

About 1 cup fresh brussels sprout leaves

8 ounces peppered bacon, cooked and crumbled

To prepare the goat cheese-ranch dressing: Add egg yolks and 1 tablespoon buttermilk to the bowl of food processor. Turn on, then slowly drizzle in oil as the mixture is pureed. Thin with remaining buttermilk if needed to create a pourable consistency.

Add green onion tops and chèvre and puree; season with salt to taste. Add parsley and black pepper and pulse just to combine. The dressing should have the consistency of a thick mayonnaise.

To prepare the salad: Preheat 2 inches of oil in a deep fryer or deep saucepan to 375°F. Fry brussels sprouts for 1–2 minutes, depending on size, until golden brown and tender. Drain well and season with lemon juice and salt to taste. Toss with radishes, fresh brussels sprout leaves, and bacon.

To serve: Place a large spoonful of the dressing on the plate. Top with the brussels sprouts mixture.

ALAMO DRAFTHOUSE RITZ

320 EAST 6TH STREET
AUSTIN, TX 78701
(512) 476-1320
HTTP://DRAFTHOUSE.COM/AUSTIN
FOUNDER: TIM LEAGUE
EXECUTIVE CHEF: JOHN BULLINGTON

No summary of Austin's food culture would be complete without a mention of the Alamo Drafthouse. This innovative movie theater incorporates great food and drinks with fantastic entertainment. Along with current feature films, the Drafthouse airs old favorites with a twist: Quote-Alongs allow the audience to recite lines from their favorite films together, while HeckleVision is a chance for viewers to text their witty comments and display them on screen.

Every film shown at the Drafthouse includes a preshow, themed to the content of the film or the event. Even more exciting are the food and beverage pairings that round out the Alamo Drafthouse experience. Unlike other theaters, the Drafthouse serves food and beverages to viewers during the films. The menu varies from location to location—there are five locations in Austin.

The core menu at the Drafthouse offers American favorites with a fun spin. Popcorn and candy are available, of course, but they are overshadowed by choices like My Big Fat Greek Vegetarian Pizza and the Once Upon a Time in Mexico salad, made with grilled chicken, jícama, and avocado. Burgers, sandwiches, and pastas round out the menu, along with a great selection of beer and wine. The Ritz downtown and Slaughterhouse in south Austin boast full bars, along with cocktails themed to current film events.

Perhaps the most creative items on the menu are the food-and-film-event specials. Most popular is *The Lord of the Rings* Trilogy Hobbit Feast, which includes Chef John Bullington's versions of the foods mentioned in the epic films. While watching the three films back-to-back, viewers dine on stewed coney with taters, pan-seared sausage with tomatoes, and even lembas bread. The premiere of *Star Trek* in 2009 was celebrated with plomeek soup, Chef Bullington's version of the Vulcan dish. The *Princess Bride* Quote-Along featured mutton, lettuce, and tomato sandwiches and screeching eel salad. The dishes are inspired by the films and yet are tasty enough to be enjoyed on their own.

Along with local beer and wine, the Ritz location downtown serves themed cocktails such as the Machete Martini and the Dude's White Russian. Other locations offer buckets of beer and wine by the glass, plus decadent milk shakes and brown-sugar lemonade.

Many Austinites have made the Alamo Drafthouse their cinema of choice, simply for the benefit of having a cold beer and cheese fries during the film. Others make an evening of it, ordering a full meal with dessert and drinks, all from the comfort of their theater seat. The Drafthouse is quirky, creative, and fun, and viewers are equally drawn in by the entertainment and the food.

PLOMEEK SOUP & TRITICALE TOAST

Alamo Drafthouse often pairs special dishes with movie releases. When the 2009 *Star Trek* film premiered, Chef Bullington looked to the Alamo's resident nerds to give him ideas on an appropriate dish. Plomeek soup (a Vulcan broth) and triticale toast were transformed into this flavorful vegetable soup with creamy coconut milk, served alongside multigrain toast. Recipe courtesy of Chef John Bullington.

SERVES 5

For the soup:

3 tablespoons unsalted butter
2 cups diced white onion
2 tablespoons peeled and minced ginger
2 serrano peppers, seeded and thinly sliced
2 tablespoons roasted garlic
⅓ cup dry white wine
1 pound carrots, sliced
½ pound parsnips, sliced
¾ cup water
2¾ cups coconut milk
1 tablespoon plus 1½ teaspoons brown sugar
1 teaspoon salt

5 slices multigrain bread, for serving
6 garlic chives, cut into 2-inch pieces, for serving

To prepare the soup: Melt the butter in a large soup pot over medium heat. Add the onion and sauté until translucent. Add the ginger, serrano pepper, and garlic, and cook until just aromatic, about 1–2 minutes.

Deglaze the pot with wine, then add carrots, parsnips, water, and enough of the coconut milk to cover the vegetables. Simmer until the vegetables are tender, about 20 minutes, stirring occasionally.

Carefully puree the soup in a blender with the lid slightly askew to allow steam to escape. Add the rest of the coconut milk as needed to make a smooth puree (you may have to do this in batches).

Return the soup to the pot and add the brown sugar, salt, and any remaining coconut milk.

To serve: Toast or grill the bread. Ladle the soup into a bowl, top with a sprinkling of chives, and serve with the toast.

Once Upon a Time in Mexico Chicken Salad with Jalapeño-Lime Dressing

This is a popular salad at the Alamo Drafthouse, themed after the 2003 Robert Rodriguez film, and can be easily adapted to feature sliced steak or tofu. The roasted jalapeño dressing works well with the cotija cheese and jícama, providing a spicy balance. Recipe courtesy of Chef John Bullington.

SERVES 1

For the dressing (makes about 1½ cups):

4 fresh jalapeños
1 tablespoon lime zest
¼ cup fresh lime juice
1½ teaspoons dry mustard
2 tablespoons apple cider vinegar
1½ teaspoons kosher salt
¾ cup olive oil

For the salad:

3 ounces mixed salad greens
½ cup julienned jícama
3 tablespoons thinly sliced red onion
¼ avocado, sliced
1 (4-ounce) chicken breast, grilled, baked, or pan-fried, and sliced
¼ cup crumbled cotija cheese
¾ cup crispy tortilla strips

To prepare the dressing: Roast the jalapeños on a grill, over an open gas flame, or in a hot pan until the skins blacken and peel, about 4–8 minutes. Place them in a container and cover tightly for about 30 minutes.

Peel and seed the jalapeños, using gloves if needed to avoid skin burns.

Combine jalapeños, lime zest, lime juice, mustard, vinegar, and salt in a food processor and blend until it is a smooth puree. With the processor running pour in the oil in a thin, steady stream to emulsify. Dressing will keep for two weeks in an airtight container in the refrigerator.

To prepare the salad: Place the greens in a large salad bowl. Toss evenly with 1 ½ tablespoons jalapeño-lime dressing. Top with jícama, red onion, and avocado slices. Place warm chicken slices fanned across the center. Sprinkle with cotija cheese and top with a stack of crispy tortilla strips.

Perfect Pairing

BATCHED OLD-FASHIONED

SERVES 17

Back in the 1950s and 1960s, many liquor companies marketed prebottled cocktails that only required a host or hostess to pour them over ice. They had the advantage of being both quick and shelf stable. At the Alamo Drafthouse, up to nine hundred guests are often served in one hour, so Beverage Director Bill Norris reaches back to this premade cocktail tradition for the old-fashioned on the menu. This batch recipe would be perfect for a large dinner party. Recipe courtesy of Beverage Director Bill Norris.

1 liter bottle bourbon (such as
   Maker's Mark)
1 cup plus ½ ounce simple syrup
   (page 24)
2 teaspoons Angostura bitters
2 cups water
Ice
Orange slices, for garnish
Maraschino cherries, for garnish

Combine bourbon, simple syrup, bitters, and water in a large container and stir well to mix. Pour into a sealable container or bottle and refrigerate until serving time.

To serve, gently agitate bourbon-mixture container to ensure that it is well mixed. Fill an old-fashioned glass with ice and pour in 3½ ounces of the bourbon mixture. Garnish each with a slice of orange and a cherry. For a more traditional cocktail, garnish with just a wide swath of orange peel.

CHUY'S

1728 BARTON SPRINGS ROAD
AUSTIN, TX 78704
(512) 474-4452
WWW.CHUYS.COM
FOUNDERS: MIKE YOUNG AND JOHN ZAPP

Over thirty years ago, in 1982, Founders Mike Young and John Zapp took over an old building on Barton Springs Road and decided to create a Tex-Mex restaurant. Thankfully for Austinites, they were successful, and the ever-popular and much-loved Chuy's was born.

Now a small chain of restaurants with locations throughout the southern United States, Chuy's started as one outpost, whimsically decorated, with high standards for ingredients and recipes. The original Barton Springs location is bedecked in Elvis paraphernalia, from velvet paintings to Elvis shrines. Hubcaps hang from the ceilings, vintage signs line the walls, and the vibe is decidedly casual but fun.

Chuy's has a favorite saying: "When you've seen one Chuy's, you've seen one Chuy's." Each restaurant has its own decor and feel, though all are held together with the same fun-loving atmosphere. Each location features an Elvis shrine, hubcap decor, and

one thousand hand-carved wooden fish that are created by one family in Mexico. Diners can feel at home at any of the locations, while being confident that the food is consistently of the highest quality.

Unlike many Tex-Mex restaurants, everything at Chuy's is made fresh. Sauces are made daily, chiles are roasted and peeled, beans are soaked and cooked, and the only thing in the freezer is the ice cream. Portions are generous, from the huge plates of chiles rellenos and enchiladas to hand-rolled tortillas and the shakers of Mexican martinis made with fresh lime juice. Every summer, kitchen managers from each location travel to Hatch, New Mexico, to visit Chuy's own chile fields and taste the fresh chiles and dishes made from them. The restaurant is serious about its commitment to fresh food and has honed its recipes to perfection.

The menu is quite large and varied, but favorites include the Chuychanga, a fried flour tortilla stuffed with freshly roasted chicken, cheese, and green chiles, and the chile rellenos, featuring roasted New Mexican Anaheim chiles

that are filled and batter-fried. Newcomers to the restaurant are often surprised at the freshness of each dish and the care that is taken in its preparation and presentation.

Chuy's is an Austin institution. Of course it is famous for its fresh, delicious margaritas and Tex-Mex favorites, but it remains a relevant part of Austin's food culture because of its funky vibe, fresh-food commitment, and refined recipes.

DELUXE TOMATILLO SAUCE

Chuy's Deluxe Tomatillo Sauce is a creamy version of its popular fresh tomatillo sauce. The addition of sour cream makes the sauce a bit more decadent, perfect for smothering enchiladas, Chuychangas, and chile rellenos, especially those filled with cheese or chicken. Recipe courtesy of Chuy's.

MAKES ABOUT 3 CUPS

4 tablespoons chopped cilantro, divided

2 tablespoons chopped green onions

2 tablespoons pickled jalapeño slices, with juice

1 teaspoon fresh lime juice

2 pounds (about 25) tomatillos, cleaned and roughly chopped

2 tablespoons margarine

¼ cup plus 1 tablespoon cornstarch

3 cups water

1½ tablespoons vegetable base (available in jars in well-stocked grocery stores)

Pinch of salt

Pinch of garlic powder

Pinch of sugar

1 cup sour cream

½ teaspoon salt

½ teaspoon garlic salt

½ teaspoon black pepper

Add 2 tablespoons cilantro, green onions, jalapeños, lime juice, and one-fourth of the tomatillos to the bowl of a food processor. Process at low speed until well blended. Add the rest of the tomatillos and puree until smooth.

Add the margarine to a large soup pot over medium heat. When margarine is melted, add the tomatillo mixture. Cook for about 10 minutes, until the mixture stops foaming.

In a medium bowl, whisk the cornstarch in water until dissolved. Whisk in vegetable base, salt, garlic powder, and sugar.

Add cornstarch mixture to tomatillo puree. Bring to a boil, then reduce heat and simmer for about 10 minutes, stirring constantly, until sauce thickens. Season to taste with salt. (This mixture is Chuy's Tomatillo Sauce.)

To finish the Deluxe Tomatillo Sauce, add 2 tablespoons cilantro to 2 cups tomatillo sauce and blend with an immersion blender until smooth. Add sour cream, salt, garlic salt, and black pepper. Blend with immersion blender until thoroughly mixed. Reheat if needed.

Fonda San Miguel

2330 North Loop Boulevard West
Austin, TX 78756
(512) 459-4121
www.fondasanmiguel.com
Co-owner/Executive Chef: Miguel Ravago
Co-owner: Tom Gilliland

Opened in 1975, Fonda San Miguel is one of Austin's oldest restaurants and still a favorite spot for food from the interior of Mexico. Opened by Miguel Ravago and Tom Gilliland, the restaurant is a beautiful retreat from the hustle and bustle of everyday life.

Once guests enter the heavy wooden doors, they are greeted by a friendly hostess and a sunlit atrium filled with greenery, live birds, and exquisite art. With its comfortable sofas and cozy corners, the bar area is a destination in itself. The dining room is outfitted with authentic Mexican art and furnishings, and serves as an elegant background to the restaurant's refined dishes.

The menu has remained fairly consistent throughout the years, but Austinites don't seem to mind. Fresh ceviches, grilled lamb chops, and *sopecitos* topped with shrimp and guacamole or cactus paddle salad are favorite appetizers. During happy hour, a few starters and one of the bar's fresh lime margaritas make for a perfect snack.

The full menu boasts appetizers of a creamy fresh-corn soup with poblano peppers and spinach salad with toasted pasilla chiles. Entrees include ancho chiles stuffed with chicken, olives, and capers; enchiladas with chicken and mole sauce; pork baked in banana leaves; and shrimp in a spicy chipotle-cream sauce. Accompanying salsas and tortillas are all fresh and handmade, and sauces have a depth of flavor that is representative of the Mexican regions from which they hail. Diners should save room for desserts—choices range from crepes with goat-milk caramel and mangos with coconut ice cream to almond flan and tres leches cake. Brunch at Fonda San Miguel is a spread of Mexican treats, including a few items from the dinner menu, plus fresh salads, egg dishes, and fruit.

Fonda San Miguel's gorgeous atrium, beautifully curated art pieces, fresh cocktails, and authentic dishes from interior Mexico draw in diners each evening. An Austin icon and still a culinary destination, Fonda San Miguel remains one of Austin's favorite restaurants.

Sopa de Elote

CORN SOUP

Fonda San Miguel's Sopa de Elote has been a staple on the menu for years. The simplicity of the freshest corn and chiles mixed with savory toppings makes it irresistible. Recipe courtesy of Executive Chef Miguel Ravago.

SERVES 6

4 cups fresh corn kernels, cut and scraped from
    5 or 6 ears of corn, or about 2 (10-ounce) packages
    frozen corn kernels, thawed
4½ cups milk, divided
¼ cup unsalted butter
1 teaspoon sea salt
2 poblano chiles, roasted, peeled, seeded, and diced
6 tablespoons shredded Monterey Jack cheese
6 corn tortillas, cut into thin strips and fried crisp,
    for garnish

Combine corn and 1 cup milk in a blender. Puree at high speed until smooth; set aside.

In a heavy, 3-quart nonreactive stockpot, heat the butter over medium heat until melted and bubbly. Add the corn puree and cook over medium heat for about 6 minutes, stirring constantly. Add the remaining 3 ½ cups milk and the salt; bring the mixture to a boil.

Reduce heat to low and simmer for about 15 minutes, stirring to avoid sticking.

In each of six warm soup bowls, put 1 tablespoon each of the diced chiles and shredded cheese. Ladle the hot soup into the bowls and garnish with a few tortilla strips.

Ensalada de Jícama con Melon

JÍCAMA-MELON SALAD

The jícama-melon salad at Fonda San Miguel is a brunch favorite. The crunch of the jícama complements the creaminess of the ripe cantaloupe, and it is all brightened by the lime, chile, and cilantro. Recipe courtesy of Executive Chef Miguel Ravago.

SERVES 6

1 large jícama, peeled and cut into ¼-inch wide strips

3 navel oranges, peeled and sectioned, with pulp and membrane removed

1 large cantaloupe or honeydew melon, peeled, seeded, and cut into bite-size chunks

½ cup pomegranate seeds

1 cup fresh lime juice

2 sprigs cilantro, chopped

1 teaspoon sea salt

½ teaspoon chile powder (optional)

In a nonreactive bowl, combine jícama and fruit. Toss with lime juice, cilantro, and salt. Refrigerate about 1 hour to allow flavors to meld. Toss with chile powder, if desired, before serving.

SMALL PLATES

No longer categorized as appetizers, the smallest plates on restaurant menus have become shareable dishes that are often the highlight of the meal. Following the style of Spanish tapas, many restaurants have expanded their small plate options, and diners often eschew the entree in favor of these mini tastes of multiple dishes.

At FINO, the Chorizo-Stuffed Dates (page 48) are sweet and salty nuggets that would make excellent dinner party hors d'oeuvres, and Contigo's White Bean Dip (page 58) is wonderful served with slices of baguette or raw vegetables. More complex recipes include Barley Swine's Stuffed Pig Trotter with Mushrooms, Farm Egg, Greens & Mustard Vinaigrette (page 42) and Uchiko's Ao Saba (page 61). A table laden with a few of these morsels would make for an excellent meal.

Barley Swine

2024 South Lamar Boulevard
Austin, TX 78704
(512) 394-8150
http://barleyswine.com/
Owner/Chef: Bryce Gilmore

Barley Swine quickly catapulted to the top of the "Best of Austin" lists within its first year of business. Chef and owner Bryce Gilmore has created a tiny space devoted to the best local, fresh ingredients and craft beers available. The restaurant was named for the chef's love of beer and pork.

Chef Gilmore first charmed Austinites with his Odd Duck Farm to Trailer, which was an unlikely combination of a food cart with a wood-burning stove. The menu featured small plates created from locally sourced ingredients; eventually, Chef Gilmore expanded on that concept to create Barley Swine.

With a mere thirty-five seats, Barley Swine is full every night as diners line up for a seat at the bar or one of the community tables. The atmosphere is lively and exciting, and the menu changes every few days. Chef Gilmore visits local farmers' markets weekly, then creates his menus based on the meats and produce that are at their peak. All of the meats served at the restaurant are locally sourced, and dishes are inspired by local farms. Chef Gilmore excels at combining ingredients and flavors in new and interesting ways while showing the utmost respect for each ingredient. Small plates of spiced goat are served with cauliflower, lime, and green garlic; perfectly cooked scallops are served alongside pork cheek and curried sweet potatoes.

To complement the fine food, Barley Swine boasts a large-format beer program, which features craft beers from local, national, and international breweries. Diners are encouraged to share a large bottle of ale with their meal courses, and waitstaff are trained to recommend beers that would pair well with the food. While a modest wine list is available, it's the craft beer that takes center stage here.

Barley Swine is a good representation of where the food movement in Austin is headed, with locally sourced ingredients, expertly prepared dishes, craft beers, and a sense of community among diners. The place is small and the lines are long, but the experience is definitely worthwhile.

Stuffed Pig Trotter with Mushrooms, Farm Egg, Greens & Mustard Vinaigrette

The Stuffed Pig Trotter was a feature on Barley Swine's early menus and is still an excellent example of the type of food and preparations that Chef Gilmore creates today. The pig's foot is braised, shredded, and made into a flavorful stuffing that is rewrapped in the pork skin to create a roll that can then be sliced. Sourcing a trotter with skin on may not be easy—your best bet would be to visit your local pork purveyor at the farmers' market and order one in advance. Recipe courtesy of Chef Bryce Gilmore.

SERVES 8–10

For the stuffed pig trotter:

1 pig trotter, 10–12 inches long, with skin on

2 quarts chicken stock

2 cups ¼-inch-dice mushrooms (chanterelle, morel, cremini, oyster, or any of your favorite mushrooms)

¼ cup finely minced shallot

1 tablespoon finely minced garlic

¼ cup white wine

1 teaspoon chopped fresh oregano

1 teaspoon chopped fresh flat-leaf parsley

1 teaspoon chopped fresh thyme

1½ cups panko, divided

Salt and pepper to taste

Canola, peanut, or other high-temperature oil, for frying

1 cup all-purpose flour

2 eggs, beaten

For the mustard vinaigrette:

1 tablespoon mustard seeds

2 tablespoons beer

1 tablespoon finely minced shallot

1 teaspoon minced fresh chives

1 tablespoon sherry vinegar

Pinch of mustard powder

¼ cup olive oil

Salt and pepper to taste

For the farm eggs:

4 farm eggs

Sea salt to taste

4 cups loosely packed salad greens, for serving

To prepare the pig trotter: Preheat oven to 300°F.

Place the pig trotter in an ovenproof braising pan and cover with chicken stock. Bring to a simmer on the stovetop over medium heat. Transfer pan to oven and bake for 6 hours.

Remove the trotter from the oven and let it cool. Carefully remove the skin; slice through the skin lengthwise and peel it off in one large piece. Shred the meat.

Sauté the mushrooms in a large sauté pan over medium-high heat until caramelized. Add the shallot and garlic and cook for 1–2 minutes more, then deglaze the pan with wine and cook until the liquid has evaporated. Remove from pan and let cool.

Mix the shredded pork meat with the mushroom mixture, and add oregano, parsley, thyme, and ½ cup panko. Mix together well, and season with salt and pepper.

Lay the pork skin on a sheet of plastic wrap, then place enough stuffing in the middle to wrap the skin around. Roll the skin around the stuffing and wrap tightly with plastic wrap. Refrigerate for 3–4 hours, or until it is firm enough to slice.

Coat a large skillet with oil and heat over medium-high heat. Slice stuffed trotter into ½-inch rounds. Dredge slices in flour, then egg, then remaining 1 cup panko, and fry until golden brown, hot and crispy.

To prepare the vinaigrette: Soak the mustard seeds in your favorite beer for 2–3 hours. Strain and reserve the soaked seeds.

In a bowl, whisk together the strained mustard seeds, shallot, chives, sherry vinegar, and mustard powder. Slowly drizzle in olive oil while whisking to emulsify the dressing. Season to taste with salt and pepper.

To prepare the farm eggs: Cook the eggs in their shells in a 145°F water bath for 1 hour. Crack each egg into a bowl and strain the extra water before plating (it should end up with a soft, runny yolk and firm outside). Finish with a light sprinkle of sea salt.

To serve: Lightly dress the greens with the mustard vinaigrette. Place a slice or two of the pan-fried stuffed pig trotter on each plate and garnish with the dressed greens, cooked farm egg, and an extra drizzle of the vinaigrette.

Quick-Grilled Scallop with White Asparagus Broth & Paprika Potatoes

Scallops are often featured on Barley Swine's menu, though the accompaniments change with the seasons. For this spring dish, white asparagus provides a delicate and fresh base for the grilled scallops, while crispy fried potatoes add a nice crunch. Recipe courtesy of Chef Bryce Gilmore.

SERVES 5

For the white asparagus broth:

4 tablespoons (½ stick) unsalted butter
½ yellow onion, sliced
3 cloves garlic, sliced
1 leek, sliced
Pinch of salt
1 bunch white asparagus, cut into 1-inch pieces
1 small Yukon Gold potato, peeled and cut into large dice
1 ½ quarts (6 cups) milk

For the grilled scallops:

Salt and pepper to taste
10 bay scallops
¼ bunch parsley, leaves sliced into chiffonade
½ red onion, thinly sliced
Juice of 2 lemons
½ cup olive oil

For the paprika potatoes:

1 large russet potato
Canola, peanut, or other high-temperature oil, for frying
1 tablespoon smoked paprika
Salt to taste

To prepare the asparagus broth: Heat the butter in a large saucepan over low heat. Add the onion, garlic, leek, and a pinch of salt, and sweat until soft. Add the white asparagus, Yukon Gold potato, and milk. Simmer until the potato and asparagus are cooked. Puree and strain.

To prepare the grilled scallops: Season the scallops with salt and pepper and grill over high heat just to mark them; remove from the heat while they are still raw. Slice the scallops thinly from top to bottom and toss with the parsley, red onion, lemon juice, and olive oil.

To prepare the potatoes: Slice the russet potato into very thin slices, creating bite-size chips. Rinse with water and pat dry. Heat oil in a deep saucepan to 350°F. Fry the potatoes in batches until golden brown. Toss with smoked paprika and salt to taste.

To finish: Pour ¾ cup broth in a bowl and garnish with the scallop salad and potato chips. Broth can be served warm or cold.

FINO Restaurant Patio & Bar

2905 San Gabriel Street, Suite 200
Austin, TX 78705
(512) 474-2908
www.finoaustin.com
Owners: Emmett and Lisa Fox

With its second-story patio lined with wooden shades, FINO Restaurant Patio & Bar is an Austin favorite for happy hours and dinners with friends. Owners Emmett and Lisa Fox opened FINO in 2005, wanting to re-create the dishes and atmosphere that they encountered in their travels to the Mediterranean.

FINO's patio is both relaxing and elegant, while the interior is divided into a dining room and the slightly more casual bar area. Diners will feel welcome wherever they choose to sit, and service is excellent throughout the restaurant.

In keeping with the Mediterranean theme, the dinner menu focuses on small plates and shareable items such as dips with pita bread (like baba ghanoush, hummus, and tzatziki), anchovy-stuffed olives, and blistered shishito peppers. Diners can also share salads of roasted beets and crispy *halloumi,* mussels and fries, or fried goat cheese with red-onion jam. Entrees include the popular family-style paellas, made with mixtures such as rabbit, pork, and foie gras sausage or mussels, fish, and prawns. Everything is made for sharing with friends.

Lunch and brunch are equally tempting—brunch includes house-made doughnuts and scrambled farm eggs with house-cured salmon, while the lunch menu features many of the dinner dishes plus salads and sandwiches.

Not to be ignored is the bar at FINO. It has been credited with helping to build the cocktail culture in Austin, and its current menu continues to push the boundaries in craft cocktails and new ingredients. The wine and beer lists are also carefully selected to accompany the small bites and paellas that the restaurant is known for.

Over the years, FINO has maintained its status as a relevant Austin eatery with fresh cocktails, excellent wine lists, and well-executed food. Its beautiful patio during the heat of Austin's summers is just a wonderful bonus.

MUHAMMARA

FINO serves an array of Mediterranean-style dips with house-made pita, including tzatziki, hummus, and baba ghanoush. The *muhammara* is a smooth and flavorful Syrian-inspired dip made with walnuts, roasted peppers, and pomegranate molasses. While it is perfect with fresh pita, it would also be great served alongside grilled chicken or lamb. Recipe courtesy of Executive Chef Jason Donoho.

MAKES ABOUT 5 CUPS

5 red bell peppers, roasted, peeled, and seeded
½ cup canned peeled whole tomatoes
3 cloves garlic, minced
1 tablespoon red chile flakes, ground in a spice grinder
3 tablespoons smoked paprika
2 cups canola oil
2 cups walnuts, toasted
¼ cup pomegranate molasses
Salt to taste

In a food processor, combine peppers, tomatoes, garlic, chile flakes, and paprika; puree until smooth. While processor is running, add oil in a slow, steady stream to incorporate. Add walnuts, and puree until smooth. Finally, add pomegranate molasses and salt to taste, and puree to combine.

Perfect Pairing

GHOST OF THE PINE

The bar at FINO has been integral in encouraging the craft cocktail movement in Austin. From house-made bitters to infused liqueurs and fresh juices, the drinks here have challenged guests to expand their horizons. This cocktail features a tea-infused mezcal and stone pine liqueur, two bold flavors that balance well in the drink. Recipe courtesy of Bar Manager Josh Loving.

SERVES 1

For the infused mezcal:

4 ounces Del Maguey Chichicapa Mezcal
½ teaspoon loose Lapsang Souchong tea

For the cocktail:

1 ounce Nux Alpina Walnut Liqueur
¾ ounce Zirbenz Stone Pine Liqueur
¾ ounce Rittenhouse Bonded Rye
Dash of orange bitters
Ice

To prepare the infused mescal: Combine mezcal and tea in a mason jar and infuse for 4 hours. Agitate or shake the jar frequently. After infusing, strain out the tea with a fine-mesh strainer. Pour mezcal into a small aromatherapy bottle with a pump sprayer.

To prepare the cocktail: Prepare an old-fashioned glass by misting/rinsing it with 4 spritzes of the infused mezcal. Place a 2-inch ice cube in the glass.

To serve: Combine walnut liqueur, stone pine liqueur, rye, and bitters in a mixing glass with ice and stir until chilled. Strain into the prepared old-fashioned glass. Finish with 2 more spritzes of the infused mezcal over the top.

Chorizo-Stuffed Dates

Chorizo-stuffed dates are a classic Spanish tapas dish, and every tapas chef has his or her own special recipe. FINO's version is stuffed with spicy house-made chorizo, but store-bought chorizo will work in a pinch. Recipe courtesy of Executive Chef Jason Donoho.

SERVES 6 (4 DATES PER PERSON)

For the fresh chorizo (makes 5 pounds):

5 pounds pork shoulder, sliced into strips

1½ tablespoons salt

1½ tablespoons black peppercorns, toasted and ground in a spice grinder

1½ teaspoons cumin seeds, toasted and ground in a spice grinder

1½ teaspoons coriander seeds, toasted and ground in a spice grinder

1½ tablespoons *pimentón de la Vera* (smoked paprika)

1½ teaspoons red chile flakes, ground in a spice grinder

2 tablespoons roasted garlic

1½ teaspoons oregano

1½ tablespoons paprika

For the stuffed dates:

12 whole fresh dates

8 ounces fresh chorizo (see recipe above)

12 strips bacon, cut into halves

2 cups fino sherry

1 cup granulated sugar

3 ounces Valdeón blue cheese

Special equipment:

Gloves

Meat grinder

To prepare the fresh chorizo: Combine the meat with all seasonings (wearing gloves to avoid contamination), then chill. Run the meat mixture through a meat grinder with a small die. Save extra for frying with eggs at breakfast. Tip: Before using the grinder, always be sure to chill its parts by placing them in a large bowl of ice water for at least 10 minutes. The meat mixture should also be kept cold until it is ready to be put through the grinder to prevent the meat and fat from emulsifying.

To prepare the dates: Cut the dates in half and discard the pits. Stuff each date half with 1 teaspoon fresh chorizo. Wrap each stuffed date with a half strip of bacon; set aside in the refrigerator.

Combine sugar and sherry in a heavy-bottomed saucepan. Bring to a boil over high heat, then reduce heat to low and simmer. Reduce liquid by half. Set aside and let cool. Note: When brought to a boil, sherry may ignite. Use caution; remove the saucepan from the heat and the flames should go out on their own.

Preheat oven to 375°F. Place dates 2 inches apart on a foil-lined baking sheet. Bake for 10–15 minutes, until bacon is golden brown and dates are warm throughout.

To serve: Arrange dates on a serving platter and drizzle lightly with some of the reserved syrup. Top with crumbled blue cheese.

Vivo

12233 Ranch Road 620 North, Suite 105
Austin, TX 78750
(512) 331-4660
www.vivo-austin.com
Owner: Roger Diaz

The first location of Vivo is still one of Austin's favorite Tex-Mex spots in east Austin. With its beautiful patio outfitted with waterfalls and greenery, it's a shoo-in for after-work cocktails and snacks. Vivo Lakecreek is an expansion of that, with more seating, exciting events, and its own lovely patio.

Like its sister restaurant, the Lake Creek location of Vivo features beautiful and sexy modern art, romantic corners, a relaxing patio, and fresh and delicious Tex-Mex food. Busy throughout the day, the restaurant caters to both the lunch and dinner crowds. Its famous margaritas are reason enough to visit—beautifully garnished with edible flowers and surprisingly strong, they are a happy-hour staple in Austin.

Owner Roger Diaz is adamant about using the freshest ingredients to create his version of classic Tex-Mex dishes. Nachos are topped with sprouts and pico de gallo, and seared queso fresco is topped with chipotle cranberry compote and raspberry puree. The tortilla soup is made from a family recipe with a flavorful broth, tender shredded chicken, avocado, and tortilla strips. Along with excellent enchiladas, chiles rellenos, and tacos, Vivo specializes in the puffy taco— homemade corn tortillas that are fried until puffy, then stuffed with fillings ranging from beef picadillo to tofu. A large selection of tequilas is available, as well as imported beers and cocktails.

In keeping with its romantic, sensual theme, Vivo gifts all female diners with a beautiful rose at the end of the meal. From its greenery and waterfalls to its cocktails and sumptuous dishes, Vivo is a feast for the senses.

Pan-Seared Queso Fresco
with Chipotle Cranberry Compote,
Grilled Bread & Raspberry Puree

Queso fresco keeps its chewy texture when seared, giving this recipe an interesting, meaty quality. The sweet and spicy sauces complement the saltiness of the cheese nicely. Recipe courtesy of Chef Paul Petersen.

SERVES 4

For the chipotle cranberry compote:

1 (12-ounce) package fresh or frozen whole cranberries
1 cup red wine
1 cup packed brown sugar
3 tablespoons minced or pureed chipotles in adobo
2 tablespoons finely chopped fresh cilantro
1 tablespoon finely grated orange zest
1 teaspoon kosher salt

For the raspberry puree:

2 cups raspberries
1 tablespoon brown sugar
1 tablespoon water

For the pan-seared queso fresco and baguette:

¼ cup olive oil, divided
4 (2-inch-thick) baguette slices
4 (1/3-inch-thick) slices panela cheese
Salt and pepper to taste

To prepare the chipotle cranberry compote: Bring the cranberries, red wine, and sugar to a boil in a medium saucepan over medium-high heat. Turn heat to medium-low and simmer until cranberries start to pop and soften. Add remaining ingredients and simmer for 5 minutes more. Remove from heat and let cool. Transfer to a sealed container and store in refrigerator until ready to use.

To prepare the raspberry puree: Combine the raspberries, brown sugar, and water in a blender and puree until smooth; set aside.

To prepare the queso fresco and baguette: Brush 1 tablespoon olive oil on the baguette slices and grill or toast them in a hot skillet until nicely browned.

Heat the remaining 3 tablespoons olive oil in a large sauté pan over medium-high heat until just starting to smoke. Season the cheese slices with salt and pepper, then add to hot oil. Sear for 2 minutes on each side, until golden brown.

To serve: For each serving, place one slice of toasted baguette on plate, then top with one slice of seared cheese. Top with cranberry compote and drizzle with raspberry puree.

BUTTER-ROASTED SCALLOPS
WITH CHILE DE ÁRBOL & TEQUILA BUTTER

The sauce for these scallops comes together quickly, and the constant whisking keeps it creamy and smooth. It is a beautiful and decadent dish that would be perfect for a small dinner gathering. Recipe courtesy of Chef Paul Petersen.

SERVES 4

12 large (U/10 size) scallops, dried, side muscle
    removed
1 tablespoon Cajun seasoning
Salt and pepper to taste
2 tablespoons olive oil
2 tablespoons butter
3 tablespoons chile de árbol (reconstituted in water
    and chopped)
4 ounces tequila
½ cup heavy cream
1 cup cold unsalted butter, cubed
2 tablespoons finely chopped cilantro

Season the scallops with Cajun seasoning, salt, and pepper.

Heat the olive oil in a large sauté pan over medium-high heat until it just starts to smoke. Add the butter and scallops, and sear the scallops until golden brown on both sides, about 3 minutes on each side. Remove the scallops from pan and keep warm.

Add the chile de árbol to the pan and sauté, stirring for about 30 seconds. Deglaze the pan with tequila and reduce by half. Add the cream and reduce by half again. Reduce heat to low; slowly add the cold butter piece by piece, stirring until incorporated and sauce is thickened. Season with salt and pepper to taste.

To serve, place 3 scallops in the center of an appetizer plate, top with sauce, and sprinkle with cilantro.

HOME SLICE PIZZA

1415 SOUTH CONGRESS AVENUE
AUSTIN, TX 78704
(512) 444-7437
HTTP://HOMESLICEPIZZA.COM/
OWNERS: JEN AND JOSEPH STRICKLAND AND TERRI HANNIFIN

By far one of Austin's favorite pizza joints is Home Slice Pizza. Upon walking in the door, guests are blasted with the amazing smell of freshly baked pizza pies, and it only gets better from there.

Owners Joseph and Jen Strickland and Terri Hannifin wanted to create a place where Austinites could get authentic New York–style pizza in a playful and quirky atmosphere. They worked hard at making the restaurant seem like it had been there for years—from the tile in the foyer and wall mosaics to the leaded glass in the windows and the repurposed doors under the counter. The restaurant is colorful, lively, and friendly, and it serves some of the best pizza, salads, and subs in Austin.

Jen worked for years in her home kitchen to perfect the Home Slice Pizza recipe, and now it is hand tossed daily and topped with fresh, high-quality ingredients. The Margherita and the pepperoni pies are most popular, but the eggplant and the white clam pies have garnered their own following among diners. Equally tasty are the fresh salads and the sub sandwiches. The sandwiches feature toasted sesame rolls, oregano, oil, vinegar, and mayonnaise, a classic Italian-American combination that complements the cold meat or veggie fillings. The culinary team had a baker reverse-engineer the bread to match the taste and style of the bread from Apollo Bakery in New York, and the result is a unique flavor and texture that diners love.

Home Slice prides itself on providing excellent service—staff members receive intensive training and are instilled with the goal of making guests happy. Each year the restaurant takes seasoned employees to New York City for a research trip, where staff members are sent to different boroughs to experience local pizzerias and bring back inspirations and ideas. The staff also participates in the yearly Carnival o' Pizza, a charity event that is reminiscent of festivals in Little Italy and the boardwalk feel of Coney Island. Hand-painted signs lead the way to face-painting booths, pizza-eating contests, and live music, and all proceeds benefit local charities.

In 2010, the restaurant expanded next door to create More Home Slice, a take-out version of the pizzeria that helps to meet the huge demand for their famous pies. Since its inception in 2005, Home Slice has become a cornerstone on South Congress Avenue and continues to perfect its mix of great pizza, exceptional service, and a funky vibe.

New York–Style Clam Pie

Jen notes that the most successful home pizzas are baked on quarry tiles or a pizza stone. With an electric oven, tiles can be laid out over the bottom rack and moved to the lowest setting. With gas ovens, the bottom rack can be removed and replaced with tiles directly on the oven bottom. With either tiles or stone, the oven should be preheated to 500°F for at least an hour before baking the pizza. Though diners can order a large clam pie at the restaurant, this recipe makes two smaller pies, perfect for a small plate or appetizer. Recipe courtesy of Home Slice Pizza.

MAKES 2 (9–12-INCH) PIES

For the crust:

1 cup warm water (about 115°F)
1 package active dry yeast
3–3 ½ cups all-purpose or bread flour
½ teaspoon salt
Olive oil, for coating the bowls

For the topping:

Approximately ⅓ cup extra-virgin olive oil
2 ounces grated Romano cheese
3 ounces aged provolone cheese, grated
4 small cloves garlic, minced
2½ cups minced clams (you can used canned, preshucked and minced from your local seafood counter, or freshly shelled)
2 heaping teaspoons fresh oregano leaves, torn if they are large, for garnish
1 lemon, halved, for squeezing

To prepare the crust: Pour warm tap water into the bowl of a food processor and add the yeast. Pulse once or twice to dissolve.

Add 3 cups flour and the salt to the bowl and process until the dough forms into a ball, about 2–3 minutes. When the dough is ready, it should feel as soft and supple as an ear lobe. Test it by squeezing some between your fingers. If it is sticky, add a dusting of flour and process until it is no longer sticky. If it is dry, add water—no more than 1 tablespoon at a time—until the right consistency has been reached.

Remove the dough ball, gathering up any stray bits, and separate the dough into two equal parts. Knead each one into a ball.

Place each ball into a metal or glass bowl lightly coated with olive oil and roll around so that the surface is coated. Tightly seal the bowl with plastic wrap to trap in the moisture and allow the dough to rise faster.

Place the bowls in a warm place (such as the cooktop of a preheating oven). After about 30–45 minutes, or when the dough has doubled in bulk, punch it down to release the gases and knead it again for about a minute.

Add more oil to the bowls if needed and repeat the rising process for another 30–45 minutes to develop the gluten.

Preheat the oven to 500°F

Once the dough has doubled in bulk a second time, punch it down again. Knead it for 1 minute, then let it rest under a dish towel for 20 minutes.

Stretch out and shape each ball of dough into a flat circle about 1-inch thick. Lightly flour the work surface and the dough, and continue do to this as you work with it if it gets too sticky.

Starting from the center, slap the dough with your fingertips, moving in a circle to the outside of the dough. Don't go all the way to the rim; leaving the edge puffy is how the rim is formed. When the middle of the dough is ½-inch thick, start stretching it by picking it up and placing it over your fists with your hands together. Hold them together, then apart, stretching the dough gently as you do. Move your hands around, one fist following the other, until you've stretched the dough uniformly to the desired size, between 9 and 12 inches. (If the idea of stretching is too daunting, you can always roll out the dough. A rolling pin is usually too wide to leave the rim intact, so it's better to use a can of beans on top of a piece of cheesecloth or muslin that won't stick to the dough.)

Once the crust is the desired size, place it on a floured pizza peel (you can also use semolina or fine bread crumbs), so it will be easy to slide into the oven.

To prepare the topping: Pour a stream of olive oil on each crust in a spiral motion, starting at the center and stopping just before the rim, leaving about 1 inch between each circle of oil.

Sprinkle the grated Romano cheese, shredded provolone, and minced garlic uniformly over each crust.

Top each pie with the minced clams and a little more olive oil.

Bake the pie in the preheated oven for 12–15 minutes until the crust is browned and the cheese is bubbling. You can go a few minutes longer if you want a very crispy crust.

Once the pie is out of the oven, spread the oregano leaves uniformly across the top and garnish with a little more olive oil. At Home Slice, this pie is served with a halved lemon on top for guests to squeeze over, but it can also be squeezed before serving. (If the pie isn't sliding easily off the peel, lift one edge of the crust up with your fingers and blow lightly to release the dough's grip on the peel.)

Perfect Pairing

THE F'HECK YEAH

This refreshing cocktail is a mix of homemade lemon italian ice and Prosecco. The italian ice is of course delicious on its own, but it adds a nice sweet-and-sour note to the Prosecco and keeps it icy cold. It's the perfect accompaniment to a slice of New York–Style Clam Pie. Recipe courtesy of Home Slice Pizza.

SERVES 1

For the Bona Fide Lemon Italian Ice:

1 quart (32 ounces) water, divided
1¾ cups sugar
2 whole lemons
Pinch of kosher salt
9 ounces (1 cup plus 2 tablespoons) fresh-squeezed lemon juice (about 12 medium-size lemons)

For each cocktail:

4 ounces chilled Prosecco
Lemon twist, for garnish

Special equipment:

Ice cream maker

To prepare the Italian ice: combine 16 ounces water and the sugar in a large pot, making sure to stir up the sugar from the bottom of the pot to ensure that it doesn't burn. Heat the mixture over a high flame.

While the syrup is coming to a boil, thinly peel the zest from both lemons directly into the water using a sharp vegetable peeler. Take care to peel only the bright yellow zest and avoid the lighter pith, as it will make the syrup bitter.

Allow the zest to simmer and infuse the syrup until it has reduced in volume by half. Add the salt and stir; pour in the remaining water and the lemon juice, stirring well. Remove from heat, and pour the liquid through a mesh strainer into a glass or plastic container with a cover. Allow to chill in the refrigerator overnight.

Once chilled, pour the mixture into an ice cream maker and churn according to manufacturer's directions. Make sure to scrape down the bowl regularly, whenever a sheet of ice is forming on the bowl. The ice is done freezing when it is light in color and fluffy. Transfer the ice into a container for freezing, packing down. Freeze for at least 4 hours before serving.

To prepare the cocktail: Add a tablespoon-size scoop of lemon italian ice to a 6-ounce glass. Pour Prosecco over the italian ice and garnish with a lemon twist.

CONTIGO

2027 ANCHOR LANE
AUSTIN, TX 78723
(512) 614-2260
HTTP://CONTIGOTEXAS.COM/AUSTIN
CO-OWNER/GENERAL MANAGER: BEN EDGERTON
CO-OWNER/EXECUTIVE CHEF: ANDREW WISEHEART

In east Austin lies a tribute to Texas ranch life called Contigo. Modeled after Contigo Ranch in south Texas, the restaurant is a welcoming outdoor space where friends gather to eat, drink, and enjoy the Austin sun. Picnic tables and bar stools, metal and leather, wood and gravel all combine to create a grand Southern porch atmosphere, where friends and families feel comfortable spending the afternoon.

Owners Ben Edgerton and Andrew Wiseheart have always enjoyed hosting and feeding friends and wanted to create a place that allowed them to do this on a bigger scale. They imagined a space where friends could sit on the front porch and drink whiskey or beer and eat excellent food, a space that was easy and casual but still focused on the details of hospitality. If the nightly crowds eager to partake in their vision are any indication, Edgerton and Wiseheart have succeeded.

The menu features approachable fare that is smartened up with fresh, local ingredients and exciting combinations. Pigs in a blanket with house-made sausage, white bean dip swirled with duck fat, pork liver pâté with eggplant fritters, and rabbit and dumplings are all dinner items full of flavor and comfort that are easily shared at the table. Brunch is a mix of Texas Sunday dishes, including biscuits and gravy made with brioche, hash with potatoes, egg, and beef tongue, and pozole with braised pork and hominy.

Chef Wiseheart has created all these dishes with the hopes of bringing Contigo Ranch to Austinites, and has done it with the intention of supporting the local community as much as possible. Most ingredients come from local farmers and ranchers, and the restaurant welcomes families with pets. It is an inclusive, friendly spot that has filled a niche in the Austin dining scene.

Not to be missed are the cocktails at Contigo; bar manager Houston Eaves has created a menu of craft cocktails featuring local spirits and fresh juices. Guests can sip on an excellent old-fashioned or their favorite beer on tap as they relax on the patio and watch the sun set.

White Bean Dip

Contigo's white bean dip is perfect for sharing with friends. The beans are cooked with sweet onions and white wine, then blended with melted duck fat to create a creamy and decadent puree. At the restaurant, the dip is topped with salsa verde and served with slices of baguette. While the recipe could easily be halved, this amount is great for a party or large gathering. Recipe courtesy of Executive Chef Andrew Wiseheart.

SERVES 10–12

1 pound dry white beans (cannellini or great northern)
2 tablespoons olive oil
1 white onion, diced
1 750 ml bottle white wine
1¼ cups (10 ounces) duck fat, melted
Salt to taste
Bread, crackers, chips, vegetables, salsa verde, and/or roasted peppers, for serving

Soak beans in water to cover overnight. Drain.

In a large pot, heat olive oil over medium-high heat. Cook onions until softened. Add white wine and reduce until almost dry. Add soaked, drained beans and enough water to cover. Bring to a boil; reduce heat and simmer 1 ½–2 hours, or until the beans are very soft.

Transfer cooked beans with a slotted spoon to a food processor and begin to puree (you may need to do this in batches). Slowly add melted duck fat while pureeing. Season with salt.

Serve with bread, crackers, chips, or vegetables, or top with salsa verde, roasted peppers, or chopped fresh vegetables.

CHICKEN & APPLE SAUSAGE

Chef Wiseheart makes all of the charcuterie at Contigo, including several types of sausage. This version features chicken and apples, and it can either be stuffed into a casing or formed into patties, making it versatile for using at home. Freeze any extra sausage for later use. Recipe courtesy of Executive Chef Andrew Wiseheart.

MAKES ABOUT 7 POUNDS

5 pounds dark-meat chicken pieces, deboned

1 pound chicken skin (from chicken pieces)

1¼ pounds fatty pork scrap (fat back, belly, or pork shoulder)

4½ teaspoons salt

½ teaspoon ground mace

½ teaspoon ground ginger

¼ teaspoon grated nutmeg

1 tablespoon black pepper

3 tablespoons unsalted butter, divided

1 cup finely diced leeks

1 cup finely diced apples

½ cup apple brandy

¼ cup heavy cream

¾ cup minced fresh flat-leaf parsley

Special equipment:

Meat grinder
Hog casing for stuffing (optional)

In a large bowl, combine chicken, skin, pork, salt, mace, ground ginger, nutmeg, and black pepper. Cover and let marinate in the refrigerator overnight.

In a medium skillet, heat 2 tablespoons of butter over medium-high heat; add leeks and cook until softened. Set aside.

In a separate skillet, sauté apples for 1–2 minutes in remaining tablespoon of butter, stirring often. Deglaze with apple brandy. Set aside.

Using a meat grinder, grind half of the chicken mixture using a large die. Grind the remaining half using a medium die. Add reserved leeks and apples, cream, and parsley to ground meat and mix well.

Stuff into hog casing or form into patties. Cook however you wish—for example, in a sauté pan with oil or on the grill until patties are cooked through. Try serving grilled patties on mini challah buns for small sliders.

UCHIKO

4200 NORTH LAMAR
AUSTIN, TX 78756
(512) 916-4808
HTTP://UCHIAUSTIN.COM/UCHIKO
OWNER/CHEF: TYSON COLE; EXECUTIVE CHEF: PAUL QUI

Uchiko literally means "child of Uchi"; this sister restaurant of the pioneering Uchi (page 190) is equally loved in Austin. With more seating and a larger kitchen, Uchiko offers a new, reservation-based location to satisfy diners' insatiable appetite for Owner-Chef Tyson Cole's innovative cuisine.

The interior of Uchiko boasts a "Japanese farmhouse" aesthetic, with handcrafted features and textures of smooth wood and red brick. The front room of the restaurant houses a bar that is popular for a quick drink and sushi. At the rear of the main dining room is a beautifully appointed, glass-lined room for private parties, with its own window to the kitchen, where a dedicated chef prepares the food for that evening.

Executive Chef (and Bravo's *Top Chef* winner) Paul Qui worked his way through the

ranks at Uchi and has now taken the helm at Uchiko. Armed with a rigorous training from Chef Cole and a unique creative vision for the food, Chef Qui has managed to create an entirely new menu with Uchi's emphasis on high-quality ingredients and expert Japanese techniques.

The menu is updated daily with the freshest fish and produce available. Specials like pickled cherry blossoms with fiddlehead ferns and lobster with strawberry, black pepper, and cilantro make the most of the season's produce. On the everyday menu, tastings of raw fish with bright accompaniments (sea bass with Texas grapefruit, avocado, and fennel vinegar, for example) sit alongside dishes of pork belly and the inventive Jar Jar Duck, a mix of duck, candied kumquat, and endive artfully arranged and sealed in a jar with fragrant rosemary smoke. Sashimi and nigiri, tempura and sushi rolls are elevated versions of the norm, with additions like golden beets and charred green onions. Pastry chef Philip Speer's tobacco-infused cream with chocolate sorbet, and sweet corn sorbet with polenta custard provide light and inspired endings to the meal.

The success of Uchiko's ambitious menu marks the growth of a young, creative community of chefs and diners in Austin who are ready to taste and explore new ingredients and cooking styles. Uchiko won't disappoint.

Ao Saba

Mackerel with Blue Foot Mushrooms, Juniper & Huckleberry Gastrique

This beautiful dish highlights the wonderful texture and flavor of mackerel. While each of the components is of course delicious on its own, altogether, they serve to balance and brighten the flavor of the fish. Recipe courtesy of Chef Tyson Cole.

SERVES 1

For the toasted juniper:

1 cup dried juniper berries

For the pickled blue foot mushrooms:

¾ cup white vinegar
¾ cup sugar
1½ cups water
4 ounces blue foot mushrooms (available at specialty markets), cleaned and quartered

For the huckleberry gastrique:

1 cup water
2 tablespoons *yukari* (dried red shiso salt, available at Asian markets)
¾ cup sugar
¾ cup huckleberries
Kosher salt to taste

For the saba shime (marinated mackerel):

8 tablespoons salt
1 (4-ounce) mackerel fillet
2 ounces dried kombu (seaweed variety used in Asian cooking)
1 cup rice wine vinegar

Borage blossoms, for garnish

To prepare the toasted juniper: Preheat the oven to 325°F. Place the berries on a baking sheet and toast in oven for 10–15 minutes. Remove from oven and let cool a bit. Crush the berries with the back of a knife, creating a rough crumb texture. Reserve in an airtight container.

To prepare the blue foot mushrooms: Combine vinegar, sugar, and water in a medium saucepan and bring to a boil over high heat; allow sugar to dissolve. Add mushrooms to liquid; remove from heat and let cool. Set aside.

To prepare the huckleberry gastrique: Combine the water, yukari, and sugar in a small saucepan. Bring to a boil over high heat, stirring to mix well. Reduce heat and simmer for about 7–10 minutes, until the liquid coats the back of a spoon and is reduced by one-third. Remove from heat and stir in the huckleberries. Season with salt to taste and let cool to room temperature. Set aside.

To prepare the saba shime: Add salt to a shallow bowl; place the mackerel fillet, flesh side down, in salt so that it covers the entire flesh side of the fish. Let the fillet cure for 30 minutes.

Remove fillet from salt and carefully rinse off the salt with cold water. Be gentle with the fillet, as mackerel is very fragile. Set aside.

Using a damp cloth, wipe off the white sediment from the kombu. In a small container, combine kombu with rice wine vinegar. Add mackerel fillet and soak the fish for 1 hour.

Remove fish from vinegar mixture and place skin side up onto a clean, lint-free kitchen towel. Gently peel off the outer skin and score the skin side in a small crisscross pattern and refrigerate until just before serving.

To finish: Grill the mackerel on a preheated grill until cooked through, about 4 minutes on each side.

Place the mushrooms on the grill and sear lightly.

To serve: Drizzle huckleberry gastrique on a large plate. Place the grilled mushrooms off center. Place seared fish across the center of the plate, and garnish with borage blossoms and three small piles of toasted juniper.

YOKAI BERRY

This dish is a surprising and delicious fusion of several superfoods—kale, quinoa, salmon, citrus, and green tea. The crunchy candied quinoa and fried kale add a contrasting texture to the smooth salmon and juicy berries. Recipe courtesy of Chef Tyson Cole.

SERVES 1

For the yuzu dashi:

3¾ cups yuzu juice (available at Asian markets)
2 tablespoons *hon dashi* (bonito fish-stock powder, available at Asian markets)
1 cup plus 2 tablespoons sugar

For the candied red quinoa:

1 cup water
¼ cup red quinoa
2 cups simple syrup (page 24)
Canola or vegetable oil, for frying
Salt to taste

For the green-tea oil:

2 tablespoons dried green tea (matcha powder or loose green tea works well)
¼ cup soy oil
¼ cup extra-virgin olive oil

For the fried and blanched kale:

4 leaves lacinato kale, stems removed
Canola or vegetable oil, for frying

For assembly:

2 ounces farm-raised salmon, diced into small cubes
3 tablespoons Asian pear, diced into small cubes
1/8 teaspoon minced garlic
1 tablespoon (about 7) blueberries

To prepare the yuzu dashi: Whisk all ingredients until well combined. Chill until serving time.

To prepare the candied red quinoa: Add water to a small saucepan and bring to a boil. Add quinoa and simmer over medium heat until quinoa is soft, about 12–15 minutes. Drain.

In a small saucepan, combine quinoa and simple syrup. Bring just to a boil; reduce heat and simmer for 30 minutes. Strain and rinse quinoa. Shake off as much water as possible.

Heat 2 inches of canola oil to 350°F in a deep saucepan. Add the quinoa and keep stirring; fry until golden and crisp. Scoop the quinoa out of the oil with a fine mesh strainer or spoon, and place on paper towels. Season with salt.

To prepare the green-tea oil: Add green tea to a 1-cup measuring cup. Heat the soy oil briefly in a pan and pour over green tea. Mix well, and steep for 1 hour. After an hour, add enough room-temperature olive oil to make ½ cup. Strain through a coffee filter and set aside.

To prepare the fried kale: Heat an inch of canola or vegetable oil in a small frying pan to 320°F. Fry 2 kale leaves just until crispy. The kale should be light and green; if the oil is too hot or if the kale is fried too long, it will take on a brown tint. Scoop the kale out of the oil and set on paper towels to drain.

To prepare the blanched kale: Bring a small saucepan of salted water to a boil. Blanch the remaining 2 kale leaves for just a minute, until color is bright green, then shock in a bowl of ice water. Drain.

To assemble: Toss the salmon and pear with the garlic, ¼ teaspoon prepared green-tea oil, and 1½ teaspoons prepared yuzu dashi in a small bowl.

In another small bowl, dress the blanched kale with a light drizzle of yuzu dashi.

To serve: Lay the blanched kale leaves near the center of a plate. Spoon the salmon and pear mixture in a line down the center, and scatter the blueberries on top. Lightly drizzle green-tea oil over all and garnish with fried kale.

Haddingtons

601 West 6th Street
Austin, TX 78701
(512) 992-0204
www.haddingtonsrestaurant.com
Owner: Michael Polombo

Haddingtons is a warm and inviting American tavern that brings many diners, beer lovers, and cocktail fanatics to West 6th Street. Named for a ship captained by owner Michael Polombo's great-grandfather, the restaurant is a beautiful interpretation of tavern and pub culture in America.

The restaurant boasts two bars—the main bar in the dining room and a smaller, more intimate bar tucked away in the Fox Tavern, a darker and cozier dining area. There are dark booths and large tables, plush bench seats, and a patio looking out over busy 6th Street. Each area is beautifully decorated with wood panels, stained glass, mounted animals, and paintings. The atmosphere throughout the restaurant is convivial and relaxed, an ode to the meeting places and taverns of the past.

Haddingtons serves dinner until midnight every day except major holidays, and locals wander in throughout the evening hours for full dinners, snacks, or drinks at the bar. The menu changes seasonally, though a few staples, like the mussels and the mini duck meat loaves, are too popular to change. The kitchen uses as many domestic products as possible, and adds modern elements to classic, comforting dishes. The result is a list of familiar dishes that are creatively updated and presented.

The dinner menu is made up of snacks, small plates, soups, salads, cheese plates, and entrees. It's easy to make a meal of small plates like the truffled egg custard with toast points, the venison tartare with juniper potato chips, or the steamed mussels with sage and bacon. The list of domestic cheeses is outstanding, all served with bread and honey. Entrees range from salmon with dill risotto and capers to the ham hock with black-eyed peas. Desserts are just as homey, including sticky toffee pudding and blueberry clafouti. The restaurant also can also prepare whole animal roasts (pig, lamb, or fish) for private events.

Brunch is also hearty, with buttermilk pancakes and whipped peanut butter, fried chicken eggs Benedict, and foie gras biscuits and gravy. Just as important are the excellent libations available at Haddingtons. The crafted cocktails combine the best spirits with fresh juices and house-made mixers, while the beer list features a fun variety of brews. Whether for a dinner with friends or a few drinks and snacks at the bar, it's worth stopping in to enjoy the atmosphere and inspired tavern fare.

Mussels Steamed in SarVecchio Broth with Slow-Roasted Tomato and Frizzled Leek

This dish showcases not only the fresh steamed mussels, but also the flavorful broth made with SarVecchio, an American-style Parmesan cheese made in Wisconsin. The sweet roasted tomatoes and crunchy fried leeks add color and texture to the dish. Recipe courtesy of Chef Jacob Weaver.

MAKES 5 TO 6 SERVINGS.

For Slow Roasted Tomato:

5 pounds Roma tomatoes, cored, cut in half laterally, seeded
1 large garlic clove, chopped
2½ tablespoons extra-virgin olive oil
8 sprigs of thyme
Kosher salt to taste

For the SarVecchio Broth:

4 cups chicken broth
3 garlic cloves, crushed
1 medium carrot, peeled and sliced into ¼-inch thick rounds
4 ounces SarVecchio or Parmesan cheese, cut into 2-inch cubes
Salt to taste

For the Frizzled Leeks:

2 large leeks, white parts only
1 cup all-purpose flour
1 teaspoon smoked paprika
Peanut or vegetable oil, for frying
Kosher salt to taste

For the Mussels:

2 pounds PEI mussels, cleaned, beard removed
¾ cup dry white wine
¼ cup chopped fresh basil

To prepare the slow roasted tomato: Preheat oven to 250°F.

Toss the tomatoes with the remaining ingredients, making sure the garlic is evenly distributed. Lay the tomatoes out on a sheet pan lined with parchment paper, cut-side up. Cover with another sheet of parchment paper or a Silpat.

Bake for about 6 hours, turning the tray every hour. Remove the tomatoes from the corners of the tray first, as they will be first to roast.

To make the SarVecchio broth: Combine the chicken stock, garlic, and carrot in a large pot and bring to a simmer. Add the cheese, and simmer until the carrots are soft, about 10 minutes.

Pour the mixture into a blender and cover with the lid slightly askew to let steam escape. Puree, in batches if the blender is too full, until smooth. Strain the broth through a chinois or fine-mesh strainer twice, pushing the mixture through with a wooden spoon to get as much broth as possible.

To make the frizzled leeks: Cut each leek in half lengthwise and rinse well. Separate the layers of the leeks, and slice lengthwise as thinly as possible. Slightly dampen the sliced leeks with a few drops of water.

Combine flour and smoked paprika in a bowl. Toss the leeks with the seasoned flour until lightly coated.

Heat three inches of oil in a deep skillet or deep-fryer to 300°F. Add the leeks and fry, tossing every 15 seconds, until they are golden brown. Remove leeks and transfer to a sheet pan lined with paper towels to drain. Season to taste with salt.

To make the mussels: Set a deep skillet on medium-high heat until it is very hot. Add the mussels to the pan and cook on high heat until they begin to open slightly.

Add the wine and the slow roasted tomatoes. Simmer and reduce for about 30 seconds.

Add the SarVecchio broth and bring to a simmer. Cook until the mussels are fully opened.

To serve: Spoon mussels into each bowl. Ladle the broth over them and top with a pile of leeks. Sprinkle with fresh basil.

BIG PLATES

In many Austin restaurants, entrees are simply referred to as "big plates," perfect for sharing with tablemates. The recipes that follow show off the chefs' creativity as flavors, textures, and colors are skillfully combined.

For cooler autumn and winter nights, the hearty Shepherd's Pie from Buenos Aires Cafe (page 107) or 24 Diner's Chicken & Dumplings (page 98) would be great choices. Warmer weather calls for Fabi + Rosi's Rockfish with Mini Heirloom Tomato Ragout, White Wine, & Potato Nest,(page 72) or Sagra's Brodetto di Pesce (page 76). Hefty sandwiches like Noble Pig's Duck Pastrami Sandwich (page 96) or Frank's Jackalope Sammies (page 93) would be great for casual get-togethers, while the Espresso-Rubbed Sika Deer with Butternut Squash & Spinach from Paggi House (page 104) or the Vivaneau aux Raisins from Chez Nous (page 112) would be perfect for an elegant dinner party.

FABI + ROSI

509 HEARN STREET
AUSTIN, TX 78703
(512) 236-0642
WWW.FABIANDROSI.COM
OWNER/CHEF: WOLFGANG MURBER

Fabi + Rosi is a hidden gem in west Austin, tucked away in a beautiful Craftsman-style bungalow that was built in 1908. The interior is modern and welcoming, with family photos hung on the walls and dimly lit cozy corners. The front patio is simply outfitted with cafe tables and chandeliers hung from trees. The atmosphere provides a classy but comfortable space to enjoy Chef Wolfgang Murber's inspired and farm-fresh European cuisine.

Chef Murber, originally from Germany, is passionate about sourcing the best local, seasonal ingredients for his kitchen. Meats are humanely raised, eggs come from local farms, and produce is delivered to the restaurant by nearby farmers. Fabi + Rosi has its own herb garden and chicken coop in back—the chickens are fed vegetable scraps from the kitchen, and the garden is fed the waste from the chickens. It is a tidy circle of sustainability and an example of Chef Murber's commitment to being an active partner in Austin's food and farm culture.

The menu at Fabi + Rosi changes with the seasons, but the restaurant always features a balanced blend of updated classics from Chef Murber's German upbringing and new creations based on produce that is locally and seasonally available. Schnitzel and spaetzle made with local pork and the short rib sauerbraten fit easily alongside panzanella with smoked acorn squash or pan-seared scallops with parsnip puree. Italian and French classics also receive a modern twist, allowing for a small but diverse menu of well-executed plates.

Fabi + Rosi is an excellent example of how young, community-driven chefs can change the landscape of a city's dining culture by highlighting the products of local farmers, ranchers, and growers while still providing exciting, top-notch food for discerning diners. A dinner here feels romantic yet sincere—Chef Murber's honest appreciation of food is evident.

Rockfish with Mini Heirloom-Tomato Ragout, White Wine & Potato Nest

This recipe features classically prepared fish with the fresh addition of locally sourced heirloom tomatoes. Along with the crunchy potato nests, the dish is altogether bright and familiar; it would make an excellent entree for a small dinner party at home. Recipe courtesy of Chef Wolfgang Murber.

SERVES 4

For the rockfish:

4 (6-ounce) rockfish fillets
Salt and pepper to taste
Flour, for dredging
3 tablespoons olive oil

For the heirloom-tomato ragout:

3 tablespoons olive oil
2 tablespoons minced garlic
2 tablespoons diced shallots
2 pints mixed mini heirloom tomatoes
1 cup white wine
1 cup sliced fresh basil, divided
¼ cup (½ stick) unsalted butter, cubed

For the potato nests:

2 medium Yukon Gold potatoes
Vegetable oil, for frying
Salt to taste

To prepare the rockfish: Preheat the oven to 375°F.

Pat the fillets dry using a paper towel. Season each fillet with salt and pepper on both sides, then dredge in flour. Shake off the remaining flour so that the fish is just thinly coated.

Heat a cast-iron pan over medium-high heat and add olive oil. When oil is hot, sear fish on both sides until lightly colored. Place pan with fillets in the oven and bake for about 7 minutes, or until the fish starts to flake apart when pressure is applied with thumb and index finger.

To prepare the heirloom-tomato ragout: Heat a saucepan over medium-high heat. Add olive oil, garlic, and shallots; cook until just beginning to caramelize. Add the heirloom tomatoes and sauté for about 30 seconds, then deglaze with white wine. Let simmer until the liquid is reduced by half. Turn off the heat and add ½ cup basil and the butter, stirring slowly to emulsify. Stir in the remaining basil; keep warm.

To prepare the potato nests: Julienne the potatoes into 2-inch-long strips, submerge them in cold water to cover, and let sit for about 15 minutes to release some of the starch.

Heat 2 to 3 inches of vegetable oil to 380°F in a large pot or fryer. Remove the potatoes from the water and squeeze with a kitchen towel to dry them out as much as possible. Fry the potatoes until golden brown; remove from the oil and let drain on a paper towel. Season lightly with salt.

To assemble: Spoon the tomato ragout in the middle of each plate, reserving some of the ragout. Place a fish fillet atop the tomatoes and garnish with a pile of the fried potatoes on top. Drizzle remaining ragout around the plate.

JESTER KING–BRINED PORK CHOP WITH SWEET-SAVORY WINTER SLAW & WARM GERMAN POTATO SALAD

This dish reflects Chef Murber's German heritage, with a warm potato salad and a bright winter slaw. The pork chops are marinated overnight in a mix of herbs, spices, and Austin-based Jester King beer, but home cooks are encouraged to use their favorite local ale. Recipe courtesy of Chef Wolfgang Murber.

SERVES 4

For the pork chops:

1 (12-ounce) bottle Jester King Farmhouse Wytchmaker Rye IPA, or your favorite local beer

5 juniper berries

2 bay leaves

15 black peppercorns

Pinch of salt

4 (12-ounce) top loin pork chops

Vegetable oil, for brushing

Salt and pepper to taste

For the slaw:

½ head red cabbage, julienned into ⅛-inch slices

½ head savoy cabbage, julienned into ⅛-inch slices

3 shallots, julienned into ⅛-inch slices

1 cup white wine vinegar

½ cup water

1 tablespoon sugar

Salt and pepper to taste

2 oranges

For the potato salad:

8 medium Yukon Gold potatoes

1 tablespoon caraway seeds

Large pinch of salt

2 cups beef broth

2 shallots, minced

2 garlic cloves, minced

3 tablespoons German mustard, such as Händlmaier

Handful of fresh parsley, leaves chopped

Salt and pepper to taste

To prepare the pork chops: Brine the pork chops the day before serving. Pour the beer into a nonreactive dish and add juniper berries, bay leaves, black peppercorns, and salt. Submerge pork chops in liquid, cover, and refrigerate overnight.

To prepare the slaw: Make the slaw the day before serving. Mix together cabbages and shallots in a medium bowl. In a small pot, bring vinegar, water, and sugar to a boil, then pour over the cabbage. Season with salt and pepper and stir well. Refrigerate, covered, overnight.

To prepare the potato salad: Scrub the potatoes and place them in a pot full of water. Add caraway seeds and salt and bring to a boil. Cook until almost fork tender. Peel the potatoes and slice into ¼-inch discs; place in a mixing bowl.

Bring the beef broth to a boil in a small pot; add the shallots, garlic, and mustard. Pour the hot beef broth over the warm potatoes. Stir in the parsley and salt and pepper to taste. Let sit in a warm place for 1–2 hours.

To finish the pork chops: Remove them from brine and pat dry on a kitchen towel. Brush with vegetable oil and season both sides of each pork chop with salt and pepper. Place on a hot grill and cook for 3–4 minutes on each side, or until pork is thoroughly cooked with an internal temperature of 145°F.

To finish the slaw: Peel and cut the oranges into sections, removing membranes and seeds. Add to the slaw and set aside.

To assemble: Drain the slaw and place some on each plate. Spoon the potato salad next to the slaw and top with the grilled pork chop.

Sagra Trattoria & Bar

1610 San Antonio Street
Austin, TX 78701
(512) 535-5988
http://sagraaustin.net
Owner/Executive Chef: Gabriel Pellegrini

Sagra is a classic neighborhood restaurant that happens to serve up excellent Italian food, wine, and cocktails. Executive Chef and owner Gabriel Pellegrini cooked his way through some of New York's best restaurants before heading south to Austin to start one of his own. He and his wife, Sarwat, did most of the remodeling, painting, and construction to the building themselves, turning it into a warm and inviting trattoria.

Chef Pellegrini wanted to bring a family feel to the place and has cultivated a close-knit staff and a comfortable and cozy atmosphere. The menu highlights some of the "greatest hits" of Italy, along with a few home-style recipes. Everything at the restaurant is made from scratch, including the pastas, from ravioli to spaghetti. Pizza dough, bread, mozzarella, mascarpone, and ricotta are all made in-house.

One of Sagra's goals is to source as much of its ingredients locally as possible, or directly from Italy, depending on the quality and availability. Chef Pellegrini prefers to cook in the Italian style, using what is fresh and available to create the menu and letting each ingredient shine. The restaurant has its own greenhouse, which supplies some of the produce and herbs used in the dishes and the freshly made cocktails.

Pizzas at Sagra are made Neapolitan style in a wood-burning oven and are topped with everything from pork belly and caramelized onion to smoked mussels with fennel. The brunch menu ranges from polenta bowls to spaghetti alla carbonara, which has become a guest favorite. Sagra even offers separate vegan, vegetarian, and gluten-free menus, as well as nice array of Italian wines.

Also of note are the cocktails at Sagra, which feature local spirits and fresh-from-the-greenhouse herbs. Along with barrel-aged Negronis and Manhattans made with local blue-corn whiskey, there are seasonal drinks featuring baked apple bitters or oranges and cloves. The staff is eager to help in choosing the perfect wine or cocktail to accompany the meal.

Sagra has maintained its friendly neighborhood feel by having a direct relationship with local farmers and producers, as well as providing a comfortable spot to meet friends for great food, drinks, and hospitality.

Brodetto di Pesce
Italian Seafood Soup

This brothy dish is a great way to show off the freshest seafood you can find. The aromatic flavors of fennel and garlic bring depth to the simply prepared fish and shellfish, and the grilled bread at the bottom soaks up all the goodness of the broth. Recipe courtesy of Executive Chef Gabriel Pellegrini.

SERVES 6

1 tablespoon olive oil

1 tablespoon butter

1 onion, diced

1 fennel bulb, sliced

1 tablespoon sliced garlic

1 cup white wine

1 cup fish stock, vegetable stock, or water

¼ teaspoon fennel seeds

¼ teaspoon chopped fresh rosemary

½ teaspoon chopped fresh thyme

¼ teaspoon saffron

1 pound tomatoes, roughly chopped

Salt and pepper to taste

12 clams

24 mussels

2 pounds assorted fish, cut into 1-inch cubes

12 large shrimp, peeled and deveined

2 tablespoons chopped fresh Italian parsley

6 slices crusty bread, grilled, for serving

Heat butter and olive oil in a large pot over medium heat. Add onion, sliced fennel, and garlic, and sauté until translucent. Add wine and stock and bring to a boil. Add fennel seeds, rosemary, thyme, saffron, and tomatoes. Simmer sauce until tomatoes become soft. Season to taste with salt and pepper.

Add seafood in order of required cooking times: start with the clams and mussels and any firm fish. When the clams are open, add the shrimp and any flaky fish. When the shrimp are fully cooked, gently stir in the parsley to avoid breaking the fish into pieces.

Place grilled bread in the bottom of each bowl and gently ladle the broth and seafood on top. Serve immediately.

Butternut Squash Lasagna

Chef Pellegrini changes his pasta dishes seasonally, so this flavorful entree can only be found on the fall and winter menus. The traditional layered pasta dish is made even more luscious with the addition of the creamy butternut squash. Recipe courtesy of Executive Chef Gabriel Pellegrini.

SERVES 8–10

1 pound lasagna noodles
4 tablespoons butter
1 large onion, diced
1 medium butternut squash, peeled, roasted, and mashed
½ cup all-purpose flour
3 cups whole milk
1 cup ricotta cheese
2 eggs, beaten
1 teaspoon salt
½ teaspoon black pepper
2 cups fresh mozzarella cheese
¼ cup grated Parmesan cheese
¼ cup pine nuts or chopped walnuts

Preheat the oven to 375°F. Cook pasta according to package directions in a large pot of lightly salted water. Drain.

Melt the butter in a large saucepan over low heat. Add the onion and sauté until translucent. Add the butternut squash and cook over low heat until the mixture is heated through. Stir in flour; gradually stir in the milk and ricotta until the mixture is smooth. Remove from heat.

Allow the squash mixture to cool slightly, then add the eggs, salt, and pepper, mixing well.

In a 9 x 13-inch baking dish, spread a little of the butternut squash mixture over the bottom of the dish. Cover with a layer of lasagna noodles. Top with a layer of mozzarella, then repeat layers, ending with a layer of the butternut squash mixture. Sprinkle the top with Parmesan and nuts.

Bake uncovered for 40 minutes or until nicely browned and heated through.

MOSCATO D'AUSTIN

Bar Manager Justin Chamberlin has breathed new life into the cocktail menu at Sagra, focusing on local spirits and fresh herbs and fruits. This cocktail is enhanced by the deep sweetness of a house-made roasted-pear syrup. Recipe courtesy of Bar Manager Justin Chamberlin.

SERVES 1

For the roasted-pear syrup (makes 1¹⁄₃ cups):

1 pear, peeled, deseeded, and diced
¾ cup sugar, divided
1 star anise, cracked
1¹⁄₃ cups water

For the cocktail:

1 leaf purple basil
¾ ounce freshly squeezed tangerine juice
1 ounce Cocchi Americano aperitif wine
1¼ ounces Waterloo Gin
Ice
Flowering basil top, for garnish

To prepare the pear syrup: Toss the diced pear in 2 tablespoons sugar and add star anise. Lay pears in a single layer on a baking sheet. Bake in wood-fired oven (or in a 425°F oven) for 25 minutes or until soft and slightly charred, rotating when needed.

In a large pot, bring remaining sugar and water to a boil; simmer until sugar dissolves. Add pears and remove from heat. Let steep for 20 minutes, then strain and chill.

To prepare the cocktail: Gently muddle the basil leaf in a mixing glass with 1 ounce pear syrup. Add tangerine juice, Cocchi Americano, and gin. Add ice and shake until chilled. Using a fine-mesh strainer, strain into a chilled martini glass and garnish with flowering basil top. Gently slap basil top between the palms to release aromatics.

TACODELI

4200 NORTH LAMAR
AUSTIN, TX 78756
(512) 419-1900
WWW.TACODELI.COM
OWNERS: ROBERTO ESPINOSA AND ERIC WILKERSON; CHEF/GENERAL
MANAGER: JOEL FRIED

Austin is well known for its great-tasting tacos, and Tacodeli is often at the top of diners' lists, both for its eggy breakfast tacos and its flavorful lunch dishes.

Owners Roberto Espinosa and Eric Wilkerson have made it their goal to provide freshly cooked and sustainably sourced food, friendly and quick service, and a community-centered atmosphere. Mr. Espinosa opened the first Austin location in 1999. He strived to create a restaurant that served the foods he missed from his childhood in south Texas, as well as from his travels in Mexico. Since then, Tacodeli has grown to include three locations and numerous farmers' market stands, and the shop supplies breakfast tacos to a number of local coffee shops and markets.

The restaurant sources most ingredients locally, including the organic eggs and hormone-free meats. Everything on the menu is made from scratch, from the variety of salsas to the comforting tortilla soup. Not many taco shops can boast that they only cook with whole organic eggs in all of their breakfast tacos; however, Tacodeli has made using high-quality, natural ingredients a top priority.

Along with build-your-own and specialty breakfast tacos, the restaurant serves a wide variety of taco and torta fillings at lunch. Most popular are the Cowboy Taco, made with beef tenderloin and grilled corn; the Frontera Fundido Sirloin Taco, with grilled sirloin and Monterey Jack cheese; and the Mojo Fish Taco, with grilled tilapia and pico de gallo. Tacodeli's menu is large and varied, and includes specialties like slow-roasted pork tacos, chicken and mushroom tacos, and even a roasted sweet potato taco. The restaurant also offers plenty of vegetarian and gluten-free choices, as well as salads and soups.

Diners have their choice of four different award-winning salsas, from the super-spicy Doña to the milder Roja. Plenty of Austinites make Tacodeli their usual lunchtime stop, and after one taste of a juicy *cochinita pibil* taco or a shredded pork torta, it's easy to see why.

COCHINITA PIBIL WITH PICKLED RED ONIONS

Cochinita pibil is a traditional pork dish from the Yucatán region of Mexico. At Tacodeli, the pork is flavored with a citrus and achiote marinade and topped with house-pickled red onions, then served in your choice of tortilla. Recipe courtesy of Chef Joel Fried.

SERVES 8–10

For the pickled red onions:

4 cups water
2 cloves
2 bay leaves
1½ teaspoons olive oil
3 red onions, julienned
2 serrano peppers, thinly sliced
1 cup apple cider vinegar
1 tablespoon sugar
1½ teaspoons salt

For the achiote marinade (makes 1½ cups):

7 garlic cloves
1 (3½-ounce) bar achiote paste
1 cup orange juice
¼ cup lime juice
2 bay leaves
1½ teaspoons dried oregano
1 tablespoon ground black pepper

For the cochinita pibil:

1 (4½–5-pound) pork shoulder, fat cap trimmed
1 tablespoon plus ¾ teaspoon salt, plus more if needed
Warm corn tortillas, for serving

To prepare the pickled red onions: Bring the water, cloves, bay leaves, and olive oil to a boil in a large saucepan. Add the onions and serranos; return to a boil, and cook for 2–3 minutes until onions start to lose color and become tender. Drain and remove the cloves and bay leaves.

Combine vinegar, sugar, and salt in a large mixing bowl. Add the boiled onions to the vinegar mixture and stir well to combine. Taste and season with additional sugar or salt if necessary, and chill. (Pickled onions can be made 1 day in advance.)

To prepare the achiote marinade: Toast the whole garlic cloves in a skillet over medium heat until the sides just begin to brown; do not burn. Set aside. Crumble the achiote paste into the jar of a blender. Add the toasted garlic, orange juice, lime juice, bay leaves, oregano, and black pepper, and puree until smooth.

To prepare the cochinita pibil: Butterfly the pork shoulder so that it lies flat. Make ½-inch incisions in a crosshatch pattern across the top so the marinade can penetrate deeper (this really makes a difference in the flavor in the pork). Place in a 6-quart dutch oven; the pork should fit snugly inside. Add achiote marinade and salt and thoroughly rub into the pork, covering every surface. Cover and place in refrigerator for at least 3 hours, or preferably overnight.

Preheat the oven to 375°F. Cover the pork with a tight-fitting lid or wrap the pot tightly with foil. Roast the marinated pork shoulder for 3–3 ½ hours, until meat easily shreds and is fork tender. The pork will release its juices; check liquid level every hour and add ½ cup of water at a time if the pork seems to be dry. Coarsely shred the pork with two kitchen tongs, mixing in the cooking liquid with the meat. Transfer to serving platter. Serve with warm tortillas and garnish with pickled onions.

FARMERS' MARKETS

Austin has several weekly farmers' markets that are open year-round. The warm climate makes for a long growing season, so that farmers have produce to offer throughout the year.

The largest markets are the Barton Creek Farmers Market on Saturday, (www.bartoncreekfarmersmarket.org/), the HOPE Farmers Market on Sunday (www.hopefarmersmarket.org/), and those run by the Sustainable Foods Center on Wednesday and Saturday (http://sfcfarmersmarket.org/).

Most of the local farmers' markets are limited to nearby farmers and producers only. In addition to booths filled with spring artichokes and winter greens, there are producers of local honey, charcuterie, meat, dairy, eggs, and jams.

The markets have become destinations for shoppers and non-shoppers alike. Central areas with tents, tables, and chairs host live music and cooking demonstrations, and food and beverage vendors mean that breakfast or lunch can be had in the middle of a shopping trip. Austinites are proud supporters of local producers, as is evident by the success of so many markets in the city.

Komé

4917 Airport Boulevard
Austin, TX 78751
(512) 712-5700
www.kome-austin.com
Owners: Také and Kayo Asazu

Komé is the Japanese word for "rice"; it is also the name of a Japanese restaurant that has quickly become an Austin favorite. Owners Také and Kayo Asazu opened the restaurant in October 2011, after years of running the successful sushi truck Sushi-A-Go-Go, and a bento catering business called Deli Bento.

Their new permanent location is a small but welcoming space with antique fixtures from Japan adorning the walls. The space and furniture was designed by a Japanese friend and truly reflects the personalities of the Asazus. The sushi bar was made by local artisans and is lined with comfortable chairs for diners. Waitstaff are trained in the details of Japanese service, and diners are greeted with the traditional greeting of "Irrashaimase!"

The Asazus wanted to create a place that would become a Japanese cultural center of sorts, where they could showcase ikebana arrangements, promote the Japanese language, and introduce Austinites to the homestyle and *izakaya* (pub) food from their native western Japan.

Along with excellent sushi and sashimi, the restaurant serves a long list of rolls that became popular at Sushi-A-Go-Go. Most exciting are the izakaya-style offerings that are meant to be paired with beer or sake. Items like steamed monkfish liver, age dashi tofu, grilled mackerel, and *yaki-onigiri* are traditional Japanese dishes that are hard to find elsewhere in Austin. At lunch, diners can choose from three types of ramen with deep broths, toothsome noodles, and traditional toppings. Rice bowls, udon dishes, combination lunches, and assorted sushi round out the menu.

Komé has become a meeting place for lovers of Japanese culture and cuisine, where diners can learn about the traditions of sushi making as well as taste foods that are often served in western Japanese homes. Whether you stop in for a steaming bowl of ramen or just a few slices of sashimi, you will no doubt be inspired to learn a bit more about the traditional foods and customs of Japan.

Tonpei-Yaki

PORK & CABBAGE OMELET

The recipe for this Japanese home-style dish comes from Kayo's mother. It is simple to prepare but full of flavor. Kayo recommends having this as an entree with a bowl of white rice to balance it out. Recipe courtesy of Kayo Asazu.

SERVES 1

1 teaspoon canola oil
2 ounces pork loin, thinly sliced
Salt and pepper to taste
½ cup sliced green cabbage
2 eggs, beaten
3 tablespoons tonkatsu sauce (available at most Asian grocery stores)
3 tablespoons Japanese Kewpie mayonnaise (available at most Asian grocery stores)
¼ cup bonito flakes (*katsuobushi*), for garnish (available at most Asian grocery stores)
Pickled ginger (*beni shoga*), for serving (available at most Asian grocery stores)

Add the oil to a small skillet over medium-high heat. Add the pork, seasoning with salt and pepper to taste. Add the cabbage and sauté together until the pork is fully cooked.

Add the eggs to the pan around the pork and let cook, like an omelet. When the egg is almost cooked, fold over in half. Place on plate and drizzle with tonkatsu sauce and Kewpie mayonnaise. Garnish with bonito flakes and serve with pickled ginger on the side.

BOTTICELLI'S SOUTH CONGRESS

1321 SOUTH CONGRESS AVENUE
AUSTIN, TX 78704
(512) 916-1315
WWW.BOTTICELLISSOUTHCONGRESS.COM
CO-OWNERS: ANDREW BOTTICELLI, MATT BOTTICELLI, AND TIM BROWN

Botticelli's is a lovely sliver of a restaurant along South Congress Avenue serving Italian-inspired food along with a dose of live music. Walking into the dining room brings to mind a cozy Italian trattoria—the tables are candlelit, the seating is snug, and the Italian wines flow freely. A short walk through the dining room leads to a fantastic beer garden out back, with a giant oak tree shading the tables and twinkle lights strung about. It is here in this private oasis that local musicians serenade diners and bartenders shake cocktails. Whichever atmosphere you choose, know that the full dinner menu will be available.

The Botticellis brought in family recipes to start off the menu, and allowed their chef to create his own dishes as well. Everything is made from scratch, including pastas and breads. The Botticelli Bread is basically an entree in itself: homemade bread stuffed with several types of meats and cheeses, plus roasted bell peppers; the vegetarian version is loaded with eggplant, zucchini, tomatoes, and ricotta. Entrees include ravioli filled with local, organic butternut squash, Bolognese made with venison and cherries, and the popular Anatra Due Maniere—seared duck breast served atop ravioli filled with duck confit and a black pepper–fig sauce. A nod to the Chicago-Italian history of the Botticelli family, the Italian Beef Sandwich can be served wet or dry, with sweet or hot peppers. The menu changes seasonally to reflect local produce and proteins. The wine list features all Italian wines—the Botticellis wanted diners to experience new flavor profiles that complemented their menu.

Botticelli's is almost two restaurants in one. Some diners prefer a romantic trattoria-style dinner in the front dining room, while others opt for a casual snack with a glass of wine in the outdoor beer garden. The restaurant serves both groups well, and it remains an inviting fixture on ever-changing South Congress Avenue.

Anatra Due Maniere

DUCK TWO WAYS

This impressive dish features freshly made ravioli filled with duck confit, sautéed duck breast, and a rich fig sauce, which complements both duck components nicely. Since the ravioli and the fig sauce can be prepared ahead of time, it is easy to pull this together for a small dinner party. Recipe courtesy of Chef Will Schultz.

SERVES 4

For the duck-confit ravioli filling:

2 duck legs
Salt and pepper to taste
1 bay leaf
1 clove
1 star anise
2 juniper berries
1 to 2 cups melted duck fat as needed
½ red onion, finely diced

For the ravioli dough:

4 cups all-purpose flour
5 eggs

For the fig sauce:

1½ cups dried Black Mission figs
½ shallot, finely diced
1½ cups red wine
1½ cups chicken stock
Honey to taste
Black pepper to taste

For the duck breast:

4 duck breasts with skin, trimmed of any
    excess fat on the edges
Salt and pepper to taste

Thinly sliced fresh mint, for garnish

To prepare the duck confit filling: Season the duck legs with salt and pepper and place in a small baking dish. Add the bay leaf, clove, star anise, and juniper berries. Cover the duck legs with enough melted duck fat to completely submerge them. Cover with an ovenproof lid or with tin foil.

Place the baking dish in a cold oven, and set the heat to 350°F (do not preheat the oven because the temperature of the duck should increase slowly to avoid deep frying). Check the temperature of the duck fat periodically; once it reaches 190°F, lower the oven temperature to 190°F and cook at this temperature for 3 hours.

Remove the duck legs from the baking dish and strain the spices from the duck fat. Reserve the fat.

Once the duck legs are cool enough to handle, pull the meat off the bone, being careful to remove any cartilage and pin bones.

Place the duck leg and the red onion in the bowl of a food processor and puree together to desired texture. (If a chunkier texture is desired, roughly chop the duck and mix with the onion.) Check for seasoning and moisture; if the mixture is too dry, add a small drizzle of the reserved duck fat. Set aside while making the pasta dough.

Remove dough from the refrigerator and roll out with a pasta machine two times on each setting (largest to smallest), until desired thickness is achieved. Use this dough to make desired shapes of ravioli, stuffing with about 1 tablespoon duck confit filling (depending on the size of your ravioli). Seal the ravioli and refrigerate until ready to cook; ravioli can also be frozen at this point.

To prepare the fig sauce: Combine the figs, shallot, and red wine in a medium saucepan over medium heat. Bring to a simmer, and cook until reduced by half. Add the chicken stock and return to a simmer; cook again until reduced by half. Add honey and black pepper to taste.

To prepare the duck breast: Score each breast in a crisscross pattern to help prevent it from curling while cooking. Season with salt and pepper.

Place the breasts fat side down in a cold large sauté pan. Turn heat to low and let fat slowly render until the skin is a golden brown color and is starting to get crispy, about 5–6 minutes. Flip the breasts and continue to cook to desired doneness, about 5 minutes more. Let duck rest 5 minutes while cooking the ravioli.

Drop the ravioli into salted, boiling water and cook for 3–5 minutes (3 minutes for room temperature ravioli, 5 minutes for frozen ravioli). Drain and shake off excess water. The ravioli can be served as is, or it can be lightly sautéed in some of the reserved duck fat over low heat for 1–2 minutes on each side.

For each serving, place 3 ravioli on a plate. Slice a duck breast on the bias and fan out next to the ravioli. Spoon some of the sauce over all and sprinkle with sliced mint.

To prepare the ravioli dough: Mound the flour on a clean surface. Form a well in the center and break eggs into the well. Whisk the eggs into the flour until a dough forms. Knead dough until smooth, about 15 minutes, or until the dough tries to return to its original shape when it's pinched and stretched. Wrap with plastic wrap and refrigerate at least 20 minutes.

Moonshine Patio Bar & Grill

303 Red River Street
Austin, TX 78701
(512) 236-9599
http://www.moonshinegrill.com
Co-owner/Chef: Larry Perdido; Co-owner: Chuck Smith

Over the years, Moonshine has become an Austin favorite for classic Southern fare in a relaxing, charming environment. The restaurant spreads over a cluster of historic buildings, with a beautiful patio, the Carriage House bar, the private and cozy Sunday House, and the lively main dining area. The atmosphere is mason-jar chic, with comforting and down-home touches complementing the upscale Southern food.

Diners are greeted at the table with small basins of spicy popcorn, along with a large menu of wines by the glass or bottle and specialty cocktails. Starters include creative spins on Southern classics, such as the corn-dog shrimp and the fresh homemade potato chips with sour cream and scallion dip. The cornflake-fried chicken salad is a favorite, as is the creamy and decadent green-chile macaroni. Moonshine's meat loaf is made with lean but flavorful bison, while the chicken-fried steak is served with a surprisingly spicy chipotle cream gravy. The dessert menu offers shareable dishes such as white-chocolate bread pudding and sweet potato pecan pie. Throughout the menu, comfort foods receive star treatment with high-quality ingredients and thoughtful twists.

Brunch at Moonshine is by far the most popular time to visit. Crowds sip Bloody Marys and wait for their chance to partake of the expansive buffet. Migas and corned beef hash are served alongside King Ranch casserole and biscuits with gravy; hash brown casserole is balanced out with cinnamon pinwheels and cappuccino bundt cake. The generous spread is a wonderful example of Southern hospitality and home-style breakfasts, and it's well worth the wait.

Moonshine offers a comfortable respite from the downtown scene, and is a welcoming space for friends and families to gather and feast on outstanding Southern fare.

Pecan-Crusted Catfish

One of the most popular items on the menu at Moonshine is the pecan-crusted catfish, which is topped with crawfish tails and a house-made hot sauce. It's an elegant version of Southern fried catfish, and would be an excellent dish for a dinner party at home. Recipe courtesy of Chef Larry Perdido.

SERVES 2

For the pecan crust:

2 cups chopped pecans
2 cups panko
1 tablespoon Creole seasoning

For the catfish:

Flour seasoned with salt and pepper, for dredging
Egg wash (1 egg beaten with 1 tablesponon water)
2 tablespoons olive oil
2 (6–8-ounce) catfish fillets, trimmed

For the crawfish tails:

2 tablespoons olive oil
1 tablespoon minced garlic
8 ounces crawfish tails, peeled
1 tablespoon Creole seasoning
¼ cup white wine

For the sauce:

¼ cup lemon juice
½ cup Worcestershire sauce
¼ cup hot sauce (such as Crystal)
1½ cups (3 sticks) unsalted butter, cubed
Salt and pepper to taste

6 tablespoons thinly sliced green onions, for serving

Preheat the oven to 400°F.

To prepare the pecan crust: Stir all ingredients together.

To prepare the catfish: Place the seasoned flour, egg wash, and pecan crust in three separate bowls. Heat 2 tablespoons oil in a large ovenproof sauté pan or cast-iron skillet over medium-high heat. Dredge the catfish fillets in seasoned flour, then dip in egg wash, and finally coat in pecan crust. Add the coated fillets to the pan, presentation side down, and sauté until golden brown, about 4 minutes. Flip over and finish in oven for 6 minutes. Keep warm.

To prepare the crawfish tails: Heat the oil in a second sauté pan over medium heat. Add garlic and cook 1 minute, or until fragrant. Add the crawfish tails and sprinkle with Creole seasoning; cook for 1 minute. Deglaze the pan with wine. Remove the crawfish tails from the pan and keep warm.

To prepare the sauce: Return the crawfish pan to the heat and add lemon juice, Worcestershire sauce, and hot sauce. Simmer until reduced by half. Turn heat to low and slowly whisk in cubed butter until emulsified. Adjust seasoning with salt and pepper.

To serve: Place the catfish fillets in the center of a platter. Top fillets with sautéed crawfish tails, then spoon the reduced butter sauce on top. Sprinkle with sliced green onions.

Frank

407 Colorado Street
Austin, TX 78701
(512) 494-6916
http://hotdogscoldbeer.com
Owners: Geoff and Yancy Peveto, Daniel and Jenn Northcutt, Christian and Jenn Helms

In July of 2009, Frank opened its doors to downtown Austin, promising hot dogs and cold beer. Since then it has delivered much more than that, becoming a favorite spot for great coffee, artisan sausages, excellent cocktails, and live music.

The owners are a group of friends who brought their talents together to develop a space that is both highbrow and lowbrow, both comfortable and classy. They wanted to create a restaurant where people could stop by for a cheap hot dog and a beer, or come with friends for exotic game sausage and freshly made cocktails. Frank has a laid-back atmosphere with a definite Austin vibe.

Diners can choose between a classic chili-cheese dog or a house-made sausage, and everything in between. Most well known is the Jackalope sausage, made with antelope, rabbit, and pork, a tribute to that mythical Texas creature. Served with cranberry compote and Sriracha aioli, the sausage is juicy and flavorful.

Frank strives to provide whatever the diner needs—from vegan dogs and salads to the option to "pork" any hot dog by stuffing it with American cheese, wrapping it with bacon, and deep-frying it. Sides and desserts are equally enticing (think ice cream floats and chocolate chip and bacon cookies), as are the breakfast items. Surprisingly, Frank has become a favorite of coffee lovers, with its high-quality roasted beans and talented baristas whipping up excellent espressos and cappuccinos.

Cocktails at Frank also skirt that highbrow/lowbrow line, with takes on classics like the cherry-rhubarb margarita as well as newfangled drinks like the Red Rye, made with rye whiskey, beet juice, apple cider, and star-anise simple syrup. Your drink may come garnished with a strip of bacon or a cocoa-sugar rim. No matter what dishes and drinks diners choose, a meal at Frank is guaranteed to be fun and original.

JACKALOPE SAMMIES

Frank's Jackalope sausage has become a must-try for visitors to Austin. Where else can you get a taste of this mythical Texas creature? The addition of pork to the mix of rabbit and antelope keeps the sausage juicy and tender. Recipe courtesy of Frank.

SERVES 4

For the Jackalope sausage (makes about 20 6-inch links):

1¾ pounds pork shoulder trim, cut into 1-inch cubes
1¼ pounds pork trim (50% fat/50% lean), cut into 1-inch cubes
1 pound antelope trim, cut into 1-inch cubes
1 pound rabbit trim, cut into 1-inch cubes
1⅓ tablespoons salt
1 tablespoon sugar
½ tablespoon black pepper
½ tablespoon garlic powder
1 cup ice cold water

For the cranberry compote:

2¼ cups frozen cranberries
¼ cup plus 2 tablespoons fresh lemon juice
¼ cup orange juice
2 cups water
½ cup sugar
Pinch of salt
Arrowroot, for thickening (optional)

For the Sriracha aioli:

½ cup mayonnaise
1 tablespoon Sriracha sauce
Tiny pinch of cayenne pepper
Pinch of salt
Pinch of white pepper
Pinch of garlic powder

For the sandwiches:

4 hoagie rolls, toasted
1 cup shredded cheddar cheese

Special equipment:

Meat grinder
1 small (32/35) hog casing, available at the meat counter or butcher shop

To prepare the sausage: Mix the meats with the salt, sugar, black pepper, and garlic powder in a large bowl. Cover and place in freezer for 30–45 minutes. Run through a meat grinder using a sausage grind plate.

Add ice water to ground meat mixture, then run through the grinder once more. Mix quickly in the bowl to ensure even distribution, and immediately case using a small hog casing.

For the sandwiches, poach 4 links in slowly boiling water until cooked through to an internal temperature of 165°F, about 10 minutes. Overcooking or cooking at a fast boil will toughen the meat. Freeze the remaining links for future sammies.

To prepare the cranberry compote: Combine all ingredients in a large pot over medium heat. Simmer and reduce until the mixture reaches a thick, jam-like consistency. (If needed, mixture can be thickened with a mixture of equal parts arrowroot and water.)

To prepare the Sriracha aioli: Mix all ingredients and store in refrigerator until ready to use.

To assemble: Grill the poached sausages, then place each on a toasted hoagie roll and top with cranberry compote, shredded cheddar cheese, and a drizzle of Sriracha aioli.

Perfect Pairing

KENTUCKY PEACH COCKTAIL

This cocktail is a favorite summertime drink at Frank, when peaches are in season and lemonade helps ease the Austin heat. Recipe courtesy of Frank.

SERVES 1

3 fresh basil leaves, divided
1 teaspoon lemon juice
1 teaspoon sugar
2 slices fresh peach, divided
Ice
1½ ounces Maker's Mark bourbon
Lemonade
Soda water

Muddle 2 basil leaves, lemon juice, sugar, and 1 peach slice in a 10-ounce glass. Top with ice cubes and bourbon, and finish with equal parts lemonade and soda water to fill the glass. Gently roll cocktail by pouring it into a tin or second glass, then pouring it back into the serving glass to lightly mix the ingredients. Garnish with another peach slice and a basil leaf.

NOBLE PIG SANDWICHES

11815 RANCH TO MARKET 620 NORTH, SUITE 4
AUSTIN, TX 78750
(512) 382-6248
WWW.NOBLEPIGAUSTIN.COM
Co-owners/Chefs: John Bates and Brandon Martinez

Tucked away in a nondescript shopping center in north Austin is one of the city's best sandwich shops. Noble Pig serves up artisanal sandwiches with high-quality, made-from-scratch ingredients. Everything is created in-house, from a variety of crusty-tender breads to house-cured duck pastrami, and from quick-brined pickles to freshly whipped sauces and dressings. Owners John Bates and Brandon Martinez wanted to open a sandwich shop that did things "the right way," using the best ingredients and crafting delicious updates on classic deli combinations.

Take the Reuben, for example—Noble Pig puts a new twist on it by using duck pastrami, rye pickles, and house-made russian dressing. The grilled cheese includes the unlikely addition of pressed cauliflower, and the namesake sandwich, The Noble Pig, combines spicy ham, tender pulled pork, bacon, and provolone. Daily specials might include a roasted beet and goat cheese sandwich, or one with roasted pork and kimchee. Soups change daily and range from saffron and squash with chile oil to black bean and chorizo. Sides are reminiscent of a family picnic—creamy jalapeño slaw, potato salad studded with olives, and spicy pickled vegetables.

In addition to sandwiches and a few breakfast items, The Noble Pig also hosts monthly dinners at which the chefs can let their creative juices flow with higher-end dishes like rabbit crepinette or potato-crusted sweetbreads. The restaurant plans to expand into the space next door, where their fresh charcuterie, meats, pickles, and breads can be sold, making it a classic side-by-side deli and sandwich shop affair.

Noble Pig has proven to the community that making high-quality sandwiches does not simply entail the use of expensive store-bought meats and cheeses. The shop's creativity and commitment to making everything from scratch has raised the bar for Austin's sandwich shops and diners alike.

DUCK PASTRAMI SANDWICH

The duck pastrami sandwich is one of Noble Pig's bestsellers. Those who enjoy a good Reuben will be pleasantly surprised with the flavors of the duck, house-made pickles, and fresh Russian dressing. Use your favorite bread and pastrami for this, or stop by Noble Pig's deli to buy their freshly made duck pastrami and sourdough bread. Recipe courtesy of Noble Pig Sandwiches.

SERVES 1

For the rye pickles:

1 pound cucumbers, thinly sliced lengthwise
   (use a mandoline for very thin slices)
1½ cups water
1½ cups distilled white vinegar
2 bay leaves
2 tablespoons toasted caraway seeds
2 teaspoons whole allspice
2 teaspoons whole black peppercorns
2 tablespoons honey
1 teaspoon kosher salt
1 tablespoon sugar

For the Russian dressing:

2 tablespoons minced dill pickle
2 tablespoons minced green bell pepper
1 cup plus 2 tablespoons mayonnaise
2 tablespoons tomato puree
2 teaspoons lemon juice
1 teaspoon Worcestershire sauce
1 teaspoon Sriracha sauce
½ teaspoon sugar
½ teaspoon salt
½ teaspoon pepper
½ teaspoon paprika
½ teaspoon finely chopped fresh parsley

4 ounces thinly sliced duck pastrami
2 slices sourdough bread, toasted on a griddle

To prepare the rye pickles: Place the sliced cucumbers in a large heatproof container or baking dish.

Combine all ingredients except cucumbers in a medium stainless-steel saucepan and bring to a boil over high heat. Pour the hot brine over the cucumbers. Allow to brine overnight in the refrigerator.

To prepare the Russian dressing: Combine the pickle and bell pepper in the bowl of a food processor and pulse a few times. Add the remaining ingredients and process until well combined. Refrigerate until serving time.

To assemble the sandwich: Add the pastrami to a small skillet over medium heat. Sauté just enough to warm the pastrami; do not overcook or the duck pastrami will become tough and gamey.

Spread 1 tablespoon Russian dressing on 1 warm toasted slice of bread. Spoon the heated pastrami onto the bread and top with 4 or 5 rye pickle slices. Top with the remaining slice of toasted bread and cut in half diagonally.

DEVILED EGG SANDWICH

The deviled egg sandwich is a nice twist on the classic egg salad. The Noble Pig uses duck eggs and curry to liven things up a bit, and the stuffed egg halves are placed right into the sandwich for an interesting texture and presentation. Recipe courtesy of Noble Pig Sandwiches.

SERVES 5

For the deviled duck eggs:

10 hard-boiled duck eggs
2 tablespoons mayonnaise
2 teaspoons whole grain mustard
2 teaspoons curry powder
2 tablespoons water
Salt and pepper to taste

For the garlic mayonnaise:

2½ tablespoons roasted garlic
1 cup prepared mayonnaise

For assembly:

10 slices sourdough bread, toasted on a griddle
Sliced red onion
Romaine lettuce leaves

To prepare the deviled eggs: Peel the hard-boiled duck eggs and slice each in half lengthwise. Place all yolks in a small bowl and add remaining ingredients, except salt and pepper, mashing everything together. Season to taste.

With a small spoon, scoop the egg mixture back into the egg halves.

To prepare the garlic mayonnaise: Add the roasted garlic to the bowl of a food processor; pulse until pureed. Stir garlic into mayonnaise until well incorporated.

To assemble each sandwich: Spread 2 tablespoons garlic mayonnaise on a hot toasted bread slice. Place 4 deviled duck egg halves on top. Top with sliced red onion, lettuce leaves, and another slice of toasted bread. Cut in half diagonally.

24 Diner

600 North Lamar Boulevard
Austin, TX 78703
(512) 472-5400
http://24diner.com
Partner/Executive Chef: Andrew Curren

In November of 2009, 24 Diner opened its doors to Austin, and the doors have rarely closed since. At any time of day or night, guests can stop in for elevated diner classics and a friendly, upbeat atmosphere. While the furnishings are clean and modern, the diner is still cozy and welcoming at any hour.

Executive Chef Andrew Curren strives to use locally sourced products at the restaurant whenever possible. Cheeses come from the local Antonelli's Cheese Shop, eggs are sourced from a farm in nearby Lockhart, and seasonal produce from nearby farms is highlighted year-round. In addition to the static menu with customer favorites like french toast and sweet potato hash, there is a frequently updated supplemental menu highlighting seasonal cheeses and bruschetta, as well as beer and cocktails. Meat loaf with sweet onion gravy and cheddar burgers with smoked aioli are served alongside charred bitter greens and mussels with smoked paprika. The diner's milk shakes are legendary—the roasted banana and brown-sugar shake is a particular favorite among guests. For all food and drinks, freshness is paramount—produce is delivered daily, sauces are made from scratch, and dishes are made to order.

Chef Curren strives to provide a clean, comfortable environment, friendly and efficient service, and fresh, high-quality food around the clock. He has cultivated a service-oriented team who take pride in the food they serve and still manage to have fun doing it. Diners will be glad to find a smile and a well-prepared meal no matter when they walk in the door.

Chicken & Dumplings

24 Diner offers a Chicken & Dumplings special every Tuesday, and the dish has quickly become a customer favorite. Chef Curren opted for this weekly special in lieu of a daily blue plate special, and he loves serving his take on the classic dish each week. The chicken base is started with a fresh mix of carrot, onion, and celery, and the dumplings are made light and flavorful with the addition of buttermilk and chives. This recipe makes enough for a large family supper. Recipe courtesy of Executive Chef Andrew Curren.

SERVES 16–18

For the pulled chicken and chicken stock:

1 carrot, roughly chopped
1 medium onion, roughly chopped
2 celery stalks, roughly chopped
1 tablespoon salt

A few sprigs fresh thyme
2 bay leaves
3½-pound whole chicken
1 gallon water

For the dumplings:

2 cups all-purpose flour

1 tablespoon baking powder

1 teaspoon salt

2 eggs

¼ cup minced chives

¾ cup buttermilk

For the soup:

3 carrots, roughly chopped

2 red onions, roughly chopped

½ bunch celery stalks, roughly chopped

7 garlic cloves, peeled

5 tablespoons butter

5 tablespoons canola oil

1 tablespoon finely chopped fresh thyme

2 teaspoons finely chopped fresh rosemary

1 teaspoon celery seed

1 teaspoon black pepper

1 tablespoon salt

2 bay leaves

1¼ cups all-purpose flour

¾ cup heavy cream

To prepare the pulled chicken and chicken stock:
Place the carrot, onion, and celery in the bottom of a large, heavy-bottomed stockpot. Sprinkle with salt, thyme, and bay leaves, and place the chicken on top. Cover with water and bring to a boil. Immediately reduce heat to low and simmer for 40 minutes.

Remove from the heat and let the chicken and stock cool until it is comfortable to handle. Remove the chicken and strain stock; reserve. Pull all skin and bones from the chicken and separate out the meat.

To prepare the dumplings: Whisk together the flour, baking powder, and salt in a medium bowl; make a well in the center of the mixture. In a separate bowl, whisk together the eggs, chives, and buttermilk. Pour the wet ingredients into dry ingredients and stir with a wooden spoon until just mixed together.

To prepare the soup: Combine the carrot, red onion, celery, and garlic in a food processor and process until minced—do not puree. Alternatively, mince the vegetables by hand and mix them together.

In a large soup pot, heat butter and oil over medium heat. Add minced vegetables, thyme, rosemary, celery seed, black pepper, salt, and bay leaves. Sauté, stirring often, for 25 minutes, or until vegetables are tender. Add flour and cook, stirring, for 3–5 minutes more. Add 3½ quarts (14 cups) chicken stock and heavy cream and bring to a simmer; cook for 5 minutes. Stir in the pulled chicken. Drop large spoonsful of the dumpling batter into the soup, and allow the dumplings to cook on top for a few minutes. Serve immediately.

Meat Loaf with Sweet Onion Gravy

Chef Curren took it upon himself to create a meat loaf that even meat loaf-haters would love. He started with his mom's recipe, then adjusted it after tasting other versions during his many travels. The two types of meat, cheese, and fresh vegetables help add depth and texture to the dish. Chef Curren serves the meat loaf with a sweet onion gravy, mashed potatoes, and bacon-braised greens. This recipe makes two hefty loaves; leftovers make for great meat-loaf sandwiches, topped with red onion, pickles, mustard, and ketchup. Recipe courtesy of Executive Chef Andrew Curren.

SERVES 12–16

For the meat loaf (makes 2):

¾ pound carrots, roughly chopped
½ pound celery, roughly chopped
1 pound onion, roughly chopped
4 garlic cloves, peeled
3 pounds ground beef
1 pound ground pork
3 eggs
1 pound Monterey Jack cheese, diced
2 cups panko
1 tablespoon Dijon mustard
1 tablespoon dry mustard powder
2 tablespoons ketchup
2 tablespoons Worcestershire sauce
1 teaspoon hot sauce (like Tabasco)
1 teaspoon black pepper
1 tablespoon salt
Oil, for the baking sheet

For the sweet onion gravy (makes 4 cups):

1 tablespoon butter
1 tablespoon olive oil
2½ onions, thinly sliced
2 teaspoons salt
1 teaspoon black pepper
3 tablespoons flour
2 cups chicken stock
¾ cup heavy cream

Preheat the oven to 400°F.

To prepare the meat loaf: Add the carrots, celery, onions, and garlic to a food processor and pulse until minced—do not puree. Alternatively, mince the vegetables by hand and mix them together.

In a large bowl, mix the beef, pork, and eggs with a large wooden spoon or your hands. Add the remaining ingredients and mix into the meat until evenly distributed. Divide the meat in half and build 2 meat loaves on a large oiled baking sheet (17 x 13 inches works well—the two loaves will fit side by side on the sheet). Bake for about 40 minutes, or until the internal temperature of the loaves reaches 130°F.

To prepare the sweet onion gravy: Heat the butter and oil in a large skillet over medium-high heat. Add the onions, salt, and pepper, and cook for 20 minutes, or until the onions are tender and sweet. Sprinkle with flour and cook, stirring, an additional 3–5 minutes. Add the chicken stock and bring to a simmer; add the heavy cream and simmer 10 minutes.

Let the gravy cool slightly, then puree in a blender until smooth, tasting for seasoning. Spoon over baked meat loaves.

Paggi House

200 Lee Barton Drive
Austin, TX 78704
(512) 473-3700
www.paggihouse.com
Co-owner: Stuart Thomajan; Executive Chef: Ben Huselton

Paggi House is well known in Austin, not just for having a fantastic patio and great food and cocktails, but for its historical importance to the city. The building itself is one of the oldest in Austin. It served as an ice manufacturing company and an inn for travelers headed south to Mexico—it even hosted Confederate general Robert E. Lee on one of his trips. Back then, the inn was the perfect spot to rest and be well taken care of, and Paggi House has strived to keep that spirit going today.

The building has been renovated with modern features while still keeping the old charm of the inn. Dining rooms inside are warm and cozy, with plush chairs and dark woods. The front patio provides a beautiful view of the Austin skyline, while the back patio houses a well-stocked bar and plenty of comfortable seating. Nighttime at Paggi House is magical—string lights and candles provide a warm and romantic glow.

The food at Paggi House highlights locally grown produce and proteins, cooked with a classical technique to allow the quality of each ingredient to shine. Dishes range from grilled local quail with butternut squash risotto to tea-brined duck breast with quinoa and asparagus. Many guests choose to lounge on the patio and snack on roasted shishito peppers or a cheese plate while enjoying a glass of wine or a specialty cocktail. The restaurant has an extensive wine list and employs knowledgeable bar staff who can recommend the perfect glass of wine or a new cocktail.

Paggi House strives to create a comfortable, warm, and social atmosphere where Austinites can enjoy excellent food and wine, classy cocktails, and consistent, friendly service. Whether for a drink on the patio, a romantic dinner, or a Sunday brunch with friends, guests can expect exceptional hospitality and a memorable experience.

GULF-CAUGHT "SNOWY GROUPER"
WITH MAITAKE MUSHROOMS, HOLLAND LEEKS
& FRESH BLACK TRUFFLE

For this elegant dish, seared grouper is topped with an airy mushroom cream, truffle oil, and shaved black truffles. If you don't have a good source of black truffles, feel free to just add a bit more truffle oil. Recipe courtesy of Executive Chef Ben Huselton.

SERVES 1

For the grouper:

1 (6-ounce) boneless, skinless grouper fillet
Salt and pepper to taste
1 tablespoon canola oil

For the mushroom cream:

1 teaspoon canola oil
1 leek (root end only), sliced and rinsed under
　　cold water
1 shallot, minced
3 ounces maitake mushrooms, stemmed
　　and cleaned
Salt and pepper to taste
1 cup whipping cream

¼ teaspoon white truffle oil, for serving
2 grams fresh black truffle, for serving (optional)

To prepare the grouper: Season the fillet with salt and pepper. Heat an ovenproof sauté pan over medium-high heat, and add oil. When pan is fully heated, place fish in pan, presentation side down, and cook until it starts to caramelize, about 2 minutes. Flip the fish and either cook in the pan for 2 more minutes for thin fillets, or finish in a 400°F oven for 3–4 minutes for thick fillets, until medium-well (firm to the touch on all sides).

To prepare the mushroom cream: Heat the oil in a sauté pan over medium heat, and add the leeks and shallots. Cook just until translucent. Add the mushrooms and cook for about 4 minutes more. Season with salt and pepper to taste, and keep warm.

Whip the cream to stiff peaks, then fold in a pinch of salt. Gently fold about ½ cup salted, whipped cream into the mushroom-leek mixture, leaving a few large bits of cream visible.

To serve: Place the seared fish in the center of the plate. Spoon some of the cream mixture over the fish, drizzle with truffle oil, and garnish with thinly sliced black truffles.

Espresso-Rubbed Sika Deer with Butternut Squash & Spinach

The star of this recipe is the flavorful seared venison, but the bright colors of the butternut squash, spinach, and pomegranate sauce make the dish unforgettable. Recipe courtesy of Executive Chef Ben Huselton.

SERVES 1

For the sika deer:

6 ounces sika venison loin, cleaned
Salt and pepper to taste
½ cup finely ground espresso
1 tablespoon canola oil, olive oil, or a blend

For the butternut squash:

1 medium butternut squash, peeled, seeded,
    and cut into 2-inch cubes
3 ounces (6 tablespoons) butter
1 tablespoon chopped fresh sage
Salt and pepper to taste

For the spinach:

1 teaspoon canola oil
1 teaspoon minced shallots
1 teaspoon minced garlic
1½ cups baby spinach
Salt and pepper to taste
½ lemon, for squeezing

For the pomegranate sauce:

1 cup venison or veal demi-glace (or substitute
    reduced no-sodium beef or veal stock)
½ teaspoon apple cider vinegar
¼ cup pomegranate juice

2 tablespoons pomegranate seeds, for serving

Special equipment:

Food mill

To prepare the venison: Season the loin with salt and pepper. Dredge in espresso powder to coat.

Heat the oil in a sauté pan over medium heat. When hot, add the venison loin and sear on all sides. Cook until medium rare (130°F in the center). Remove from the heat and let rest.

To prepare the butternut squash: Place the squash in a pot of cold, salted water. Bring to a boil, then reduce heat and simmer until the squash is tender and easily pierced with a sharp knife, about 8–10 minutes. Drain squash.

Push the cooked squash and butter through a food mill. Stir in sage and salt and pepper to taste; keep warm.

To prepare the spinach: Heat the oil in a sauté pan over medium heat. Add the shallots and garlic and cook 2 minutes, or until just softened. Add the spinach and cook until just wilted. Season with salt, pepper, and a splash of lemon juice. Keep warm.

To prepare the pomegranate sauce: Combine the demi-glace, vinegar, and juice in a small saucepan and simmer over medium-high heat until reduced by half.

To serve: Slice the venison loin into 6 rounds. Place 3 mounds (about ⅓ cup each) of butternut squash puree on the plate. Top each mound first with spinach, then 2 slices of venison. Drizzle with pomegranate sauce and sprinkle with pomegranate seeds.

BUENOS AIRES CAFE

13500 GALLERIA CIRCLE
BEE CAVE, TEXAS 78738
(512) 441-9000
WWW.BUENOSAIRESCAFE.COM
OWNER/CHEF: REINA MORRIS

Argentinean chef Reina Morris has made it her priority over the years to bring the culture and cuisine of her country, and specifically the city of Buenos Aires, to the Austin community. She has manned food booths at international fairs, led and participated in local Argentinean organizations, and finally has opened two restaurants devoted to the food of Argentina. Both locations of Buenos Aires Cafe are built on the memories and traditions that she has brought with her from her home country.

The restaurants have a cozy bistro feel, with dark wood accents, creative and artistic lighting, and Argentinean artwork. The Galleria location features a grand mural of downtown Buenos Aires that was painted by an Argentinean artist; framed Buenos Aires bus tickets and Chef Morris's family photos bring a personal touch to the decor.

Along with several excellent versions of the traditional flaky empanada, the restaurant serves dishes like roasted pork loin with chimichurri sauce and even a comforting shepherd's pie with beef, potatoes, and olives, which was based on a recipe

from the chef's mother. Chef Morris notes that many people do not realize that the city of Buenos Aires has been greatly influenced by European cuisines and traditions. To reflect this in the restaurant, diners can expect freshly made pastas and sandwiches made with prosciutto and serrano ham.

Chef Morris endeavors to be a responsible and involved member of the Austin community. At the restaurant, everything is recycled—even the food scraps are turned into compost for neighboring gardens. Food is sourced locally and organically if possible. Chef Morris takes pride in the environment and cuisine that she has cultivated at Buenos Aires Cafe and believes that food is more than just a means of filling our bellies—it can be a reminder of happy times, family, and home.

Pastel de Papas

Shepherd's Pie

This version of shepherd's pie was adapted from the chef's mother's recipe. The usual ground beef and potato dish is made special with the addition of hard-boiled eggs, raisins, and olives. Recipe courtesy of Chef Reina Morris.

MAKES 4–6 SERVINGS

½ cup olive oil

3 medium onions, diced

1 red bell pepper, diced

2 pounds ground beef

2 tablespoons sweet paprika

1 tablespoon water

¼ teaspoon cumin

1 teaspoon crushed red pepper

Salt and pepper to taste

6 green onions, chopped

¼ cup raisins, plumped in hot water for a few minutes until soft (optional)

Nonstick spray or butter, for the baking dish

3 cups mashed potatoes, heated

2 hard-boiled eggs, sliced (optional)

Heat the olive oil in a large saucepan over medium heat. Add the onions and cook until translucent, stirring occasionally. Add bell peppers and cook until softened. Reduce heat to medium low; add ground beef and cook, stirring, about 10–15 minutes, or until cooked through.

In a small bowl, dissolve paprika in water. Stir the mixture into to the beef. Add cumin, crushed red pepper, and salt and pepper to taste. Remove from heat and add green onions and raisins; let rest for 20–30 minutes.

Preheat oven to 350°F.

Spray or butter an 8 x 8-inch baking dish (or four deep ramekins). Spoon in the mashed potatoes to form a 1-inch-thick bottom layer. Top with beef mixture and spread to cover. Top with the sliced eggs, then with the remaining mashed potatoes. Bake 15–20 minutes, or until the mashed potatoes are golden.

LOMITO BEEF SANDWICH WITH CHIMICHURRI SAUCE

The *lomito* beef sandwich is one of the bestsellers at Buenos Aires Cafe. With a full serving of juicy beef tenderloin and a slather of bright chimichurri sauce on toasted baguette, it makes for a surprisingly simple but delicious lunch. Recipe courtesy of Chef Reina Morris.

SERVES 1

For the chimichurri sauce:

½ cup chopped fresh parsley
2 tablespoons chopped fresh oregano
¼ cup minced fresh garlic
2 tablespoons dried oregano
Pinch of crushed red pepper
¼ teaspoon white pepper
2 tablespoons salt
2 tablespoons hot water
½ cup vinegar
1 cup olive oil

For the beef sandwich:

1 (6-ounce) beef tenderloin
Salt and black pepper to taste
1 (6-inch) baguette piece
Sliced tomatoes, pepperoncinis, provolone cheese,
    roasted red peppers, and/or sliced ham,
    for toppings (optional)

To prepare the chimichurri sauce: Combine fresh herbs, garlic, dried oregano, red pepper, and white pepper in a small bowl.

In a separate bowl, dissolve the salt in the hot water. Add the salted water to the herb mixture and mix well. Stir in the vinegar. Slowly add the olive oil, stirring with a wooden spoon. Taste and adjust salt and pepper as needed. Sauce will keep refrigerated for 2 days.

To prepare the beef sandwich: Pull the tenderloin out of the refrigerator about 10–15 minutes before cooking it. Preheat a grill or cast-iron skillet over medium-high heat.

Place the meat on the grill. Cook, without moving it, for about 4 minutes on one side. Sprinkle top with salt and pepper. Flip over and cook for another 4 minutes. Sprinkle again with salt and pepper. The beef should be medium rare at this point. Remove from the grill and set aside.

Toast the whole baguette piece on the grill for a few minutes just before the beef is ready. Cut the bread in half lengthwise and smother it with chimichurri sauce (about 2 tablespoons per side). Place the beef between the bread pieces and serve. Feel free to add any of your favorite toppings, such as sliced tomatoes, pepperoncinis, provolone cheese, roasted red peppers, or even sliced ham.

Chez Nous

510 Neches Street
Austin, TX 78701
(512) 473-2413
http://cheznousaustin.com
Owners: Pascal and Sybil Regimbeau

One of Austin's landmark restaurants, Chez Nous has been serving classic French cuisine since 1982. Owners Pascal and Sybil Regimbeau and their friend, Robert Paprota, moved to Austin from Paris in the late 1970s. After running a crepe booth near the University of Texas, they came together to open Chez Nous. It has been in the same location downtown since opening day.

The Regimbeaus wanted to create a comfortable, welcoming space where diners would feel like family—Chez Nous ("our home") has become just that. Sybil brought all of the decor pieces from France, and with the printed tablecloths, vintage pastis bottles, and murals, the space feels warm and inviting.

The menu is essentially French bistro fare, with lighter dishes and fresh ingredients. The Regimbeaus wanted to show Austinites that French food does not have to be stuffy or expensive, nor does it have to be Americanized to be approachable. This was a new idea in 1982, when Chez Nous was only the second restaurant in Austin to have an espresso machine. Now, diners know they can come here for classic, delicious French dishes and a relaxed, intimate experience.

The menu features a prix-fixe option for under $30 with a soup, salad or pâté, entree, and dessert. Most popular are the steak maitre d'hotel, the confit de canard, and the pâté maison. The sautéed trout comes simply dressed with a lemon-butter sauce, and the grilled rib eye is sauced with a classic béarnaise. More adventurous diners opt for the veal sweetbreads or the escargots. At lunch, the restaurant serves crepes and sandwiches as well.

Chez Nous has many regulars and has seen families come to dinner from generation to generation. Several of the

restaurant's employees have worked there for fifteen years or more, and there have only been five chefs in the kitchen. People who visit Chez Nous tend to return to Chez Nous, for the food and atmosphere as well as for the sense of family and home that the restaurant creates.

Joues de Porc au Lait

MILK-BRAISED PORK CHEEKS

Braising the pork cheeks in milk at a low temperature over a couple of hours results in tender meat that is slightly sweetened by the milk sugars. Although the photo shows potatoes on the side, the tart Granny Smith apples balance out the creaminess of the sauce. Recipe courtesy of Chef Christopher Concannon.

SERVES 3

For the pork cheeks:

2 tablespoons olive oil
6 pork cheeks, trimmed and dried well
Salt to taste
Flour, for dusting
12 ounces brut cider
4 cups whole milk
1 bay leaf
⅛ teaspoon freshly grated nutmeg
1 teaspoon Dijon mustard

For the apples:

1 tablespoon butter
2 Granny Smith apples, peeled, cored, and sliced
Pinch of salt

To prepare the pork cheeks: Preheat the oven to 300°F.

Heat the olive oil in a dutch oven or ovenproof pot over medium heat. Season the pork cheeks with salt, then dust lightly with flour. Add the cheeks to the hot oil and brown on all sides. Remove to a plate and carefully pour off and discard the oil.

Deglaze the pan with the cider over medium heat. Add the milk, bay leaf, a pinch of salt, and nutmeg. Bring to a simmer and reduce heat to low. Return pork cheeks to the pot and cover. Place in the oven and cook for 1 ½–2 hours, or until cheeks are very tender (the milk will appear curdled). Remove the cheeks from the pot and keep warm.

Remove and discard the bay leaf from the milk mixture. Using an immersion blender, puree the sauce until smooth, then stir in Dijon and adjust seasoning as needed.

To prepare the apples: Heat the butter in a medium skillet over high heat until it stops sputtering but is not yet browned. Add apples and salt and cook for a few minutes, browning apples on all sides and allowing apples to stay just crisp in the middle.

To finish: Place 2 pork cheeks on each plate and top with sauce. Spoon apples on the side.

Vivaneau aux Raisins

SNAPPER WITH GRAPES

This elegant dish would be a great option for a small dinner party. The celery root puree serves as a creamy base for the crispy fish and grapes. Citrus zest brightens up the flavors. Recipe courtesy of Chef Christopher Concannon.

SERVES 2

For the celery root puree:

1 medium head celery root, peeled and diced
¼ cup cream
1 tablespoon unsalted butter
Pinch of ground white pepper

For the snapper:

2 (6-ounce) snapper fillets, trimmed and pin bones removed
Kosher salt and pepper to taste
¼ cup olive oil

To finish:

4 tablespoons (½ stick) unsalted butter
Pinch of salt
½ cup halved white seedless grapes
1 tablespoon pine nuts
Juice of 1 orange
Juice of ½ lemon
¼ teaspoon orange zest
¼ teaspoon lemon zest
2 tablespoons chopped fresh flat-leaf parsley

To prepare the celery root puree: Bring a large pot of salted water to boil. Add the celery root and boil until tender, about 4–6 minutes. Drain the celery root and reserve the cooking liquid.

Add the celery root, cream, butter, and white pepper to a food processor and puree; add a small amount of cooking liquid to achieve a very smooth, light consistency. Check the seasoning and add salt if needed. Push the mixture through a sieve; discard solids. Keep puree warm.

To prepare the snapper: Score the skin of the fish in a crisscross pattern; pat dry with a paper towel. Season with salt and pepper.

Heat a small, heavy sauté pan over medium-high heat. Add olive oil. When the oil is hot, add the snapper, skin side down. Lower the heat to medium; cook for 6–7 minutes, using a spoon to bathe the fish continuously with the hot oil, until the fish flakes easily. Remove the fish from the pan and place it on a plate lined with a paper towel, skin side up so that it remains crispy. Carefully pour off the oil from the pan.

In the same pan, add the butter and a pinch of salt. Add grapes and pine nuts; cook until the butter has browned slightly and grapes are lightly caramelized. Stir in citrus juices and zests and cook about 30 more seconds. Remove from heat and stir in the parsley.

To finish each serving: Spoon about ½ cup of the warm celery root puree onto a warm plate. Arrange the fish on top, and spoon about half the sauce over the top.

SIDES

The side dish portion of a restaurant menu is a chance for the chef to highlight the season's freshest local vegetables. Some of the recipes that follow could also stand on their own as small plates.

Classic Texas sides like Salt Lick's Pinto Beans (page 136), the Coleslaw from Chez Zee (page 141), or Jack Allen's Kitchen's Tamale & Jalapeño Corn Bread Dressing (page 128) are approachable and easy to pair with meat entrees. More exotic dishes, like the Northern Pork and Tomato Relish from Thai Fresh (page 139) or the Spicy Edamame from Imperia (page 134) could double as appetizers. The season's best produce is highlighted in East Side Showroom's Fried Squash Blossoms (page 119) and the Brussels Sprouts with Bacon & Grapes from La Condesa (page 116).

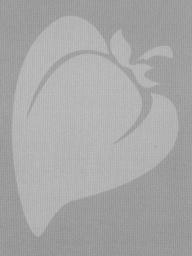

La Condesa

400A West 2nd Street
Austin, TX 78701
(512) 499-0300
http://lacondesaaustin.com
Executive Chef: Rene Ortiz

The beautiful La Condesa was inspired by Colonia Condesa, a Mexico City neighborhood known for its bohemian, internationally influenced character. The restaurant is airy and colorful, with vivid murals, artistic light fixtures, and clean, modern design. Soon after opening in 2009, La Condesa became one of Austin's premier hip hangouts, attracting diners and lounge-goers alike.

The kitchen is led by Executive Chef Rene Ortiz, who has created a diverse menu of regional Mexican dishes and inventive contemporary recipes using traditional Mexican ingredients. Five different ceviches are available, featuring yellowtail with grilled grapefruit broth or scallops with oak-grilled tomato. Crispy *huaraches* (made of fried corn masa) are topped with pork belly or crabmeat, and tacos come filled with succulent *cochinita pibil* or tender rib eye. Entrees include beer-braised short ribs, duck confit with mole sauce, and chiles rellenos with quinoa and butternut squash. The kitchen can even prepare a roasted whole suckling pig for parties—given advance notice—and it can be served in the intimate underground private dining room.

The restaurant strives to use local ingredients when available, and everything on the menu is made from scratch. Bacon is smoked in-house, all tortillas and salsas are made fresh daily, and nightly dinner specials make the most of seasonally available produce; the freshness shines in each dish.

Just as impressive is the bar menu, which boasts over one hundred different tequilas, all of which are 100 percent blue agave. Aside from excellent margaritas, diners can enjoy drinks made with habañero- or tobacco-infused tequilas, fresh juices and herbs, and house-made bitters. In the evenings, the bar and patio seats are highly coveted, as guests lounge with outstanding cocktails and snacks from the bar.

The vibe at La Condesa is always lively, whether at lunch, dinner, or weekend brunch. Guests are drawn in to the energetic vibe, and the innovative food and cocktails keep them coming back for more.

Coles de Bruselas

Brussels Sprouts with Bacon & Grapes

Serves 4

5 slices thick-cut bacon, cut into lardons

2 cloves garlic, chopped

6 ounces (about 2 cups) brussels sprout leaves
  (slice or quarter each sprout to separate the leaves)

1 tablespoon unsalted butter

Kosher salt and freshly ground black pepper to taste

¼ cup halved red seedless grapes

In a large sauté pan on medium heat, add the bacon and cook until half the fat has rendered out.

Add the garlic and cook until lightly toasted and aromatic.

Add the brussels sprout leaves and butter. Season with salt and pepper to taste; stir and cover for a few minutes, until the leaves are slightly wilted. Taste for seasoning a final time, then fold in the grapes and remove from heat so the grapes don't overcook.

EAST SIDE SHOWROOM

1100 EAST 6TH STREET
AUSTIN, TX 78702
(512) 467-4280
HTTP://EASTSIDESHOWROOM.COM/
OWNER: MICKIE DANAE SPENCER

At once a restaurant, cocktail lounge, music venue, and art showcase, East Side Showroom is a remarkable creation. The interior is an homage to the cafes and cabarets of Europe in the 1920s and 1930s, with tiny tables, bistro chairs, and black-and-white films rolling silently on the wall.

The furniture and fixtures, from the beautifully designed bar to the shelves and lanterns, are handmade by owner Mickie Danae Spencer. Tables are topped with lacquered pennies or black and white tiles, and specials are written in chalk on a metal beam above the kitchen. Cocktails are passed through a reworked barrel from the bar to the servers, and the walls are graced with pieces from local artists.

Most evenings, tables are scooted aside to make room for local musicians, many of whom play tunes with a vintage sound. The restaurant is always full, from the barstools to the lovely patio out back, and both diners and staff tend to dress artistically and whimsically.

The French-inspired menu uses local proteins, produce, and dishes. Dishes are soulful and sometimes rustic, ranging from house-made charcuterie and meat loaf with duck egg to antelope tartare and chicken-fried rabbit. A chalkboard at the front of the restaurant lists local farmers and ranchers whose products are featured on the menu—the Showroom is passionate about building a sense of community among diners and food producers. The menu introduces people to the taste of real grass-fed beef or venison and reflects a strong commitment to local growers.

East Side Showroom has become a destination in Austin for cocktail lovers as well. Bartenders are comfortable mixing classics like Moscow mules and Pimm's cups, but they are equally at home creating new drinks with fresh juices, specialty liqueurs, and top-quality spirits. From atmosphere to food, from cocktails to entertainment, East Side Showroom has it all.

Fried Squash Blossoms

The stuffed squash blossoms are beautiful once fried to a light golden brown. Two of these would be a nice side dish, or they can be plated on their own as pictured for an appetizer. Recipe courtesy of Executive Chef Sonya Coté.

SERVES 8

For the goat ricotta (makes about 2 cups ricotta):

2 quarts whole goat milk
¼ cup freshly squeezed lemon juice
Kosher salt to taste

For the filling:

1½ teaspoons roasted garlic
Pinch of salt
Pinch of white pepper
Pinch of nutmeg
1 cup whole milk cow ricotta
1 cup goat ricotta (recipe above)
1 cup shredded Parmesan

For the batter:

1 cup flour
½ cup cornstarch
Pinch of salt
Pinch of black pepper
1 cup milk

For the fried blossoms:

16 squash blossoms
Peanut oil, for frying

2 cups prepared marinara
½ cup thinly sliced basil (chiffonade), for garnish
Shaved Parmesan, for garnish

Special equipment:

Cheesecloth

To prepare the goat ricotta: Heat the goat milk in a large saucepan over medium heat to 200°F. Slowly add the lemon juice. Bring the temperature back up to 200°F. Cook, stirring occasionally, until the solids separate from the whey, about 30 minutes.

Remove the saucepan from the heat, cover, and let rest at room temperature for 15 minutes.

Line a colander with a large square of very fine cheesecloth and place over a large bowl. Pour the goat milk mixture over the cheesecloth. Tie the four corners of the cheesecloth together and hang over the colander to drain for 1 hour.

After the ricotta has drained, discard the liquid in the bowl. Transfer the drained ricotta to a bowl and break up the curds. Stir and add salt to taste. The goat ricotta will keep, refrigerated, for up to 7 days.

To prepare the filling: Combine all ingredients in a large bowl; mix thoroughly and set aside.

To prepare the batter: Whisk together all ingredients. Set aside.

Stuff each squash blossom with 2 tablespoons ricotta mixture, twisting the end of the flower to hold in the filling.

Bring a large pot of water to a rolling boil. At the same time, heat at least 2 inches of oil in a deep saucepan or deep fryer to 400°F.

Blanch each stuffed squash blossom in the boiling water for 1–2 minutes. Set aside on towels to drain well.

Once the blossoms are blanched, dip them in the prepared batter, shaking off any excess. Drop into the hot oil and fry 2–3 minutes, until golden on all sides. Drain on paper towels.

To finish: Spoon about ¼ cup marinara sauce in the center of a plate. Place two fried squash blossoms in the center, and garnish with a pinch of fresh basil and a few shavings of Parmesan.

Perfect Pairing

BLUE BRAMBLE

This cocktail is light and refreshing, and the blueberry-infused gin imparts a beautiful pink color to the drink. The gin will take a total of six weeks to infuse – the berries are added in two batches - but afterward, you will have the infused gin as well as gin-soaked blueberries, which would be great made into a jam. Recipe courtesy of Head Barman Chauncy James.

SERVES 1

For the blueberry-infused gin:

1 (750 ml) bottle Death's Door Gin
6 cups blueberries, divided

For the cocktail:

½ ounce simple syrup (page 24)
½ ounce fresh lime juice
2 or 3 drops sarsparilla bitters (such as Bad Dog)
Ice
Basil leaf, for garnish
Lime zest, for garnish

To prepare the blueberry-infused gin: Combine the gin and 3 cups blueberries in a large container. Seal and let sit at room temperature for 3 weeks.

After 3 weeks, strain the blueberries from the gin with a fine-meshed sieve. Add the remaining 3 cups fresh blueberries to the gin, and repeat the 3-week infusion. After the second infusion, strain the blueberries out of the gin. Store the infused gin in a resealable bottle. Save the berries for another use, if desired.

To prepare the cocktail: Combine the simple syrup, lime juice, and bitters with 1¾ ounces blueberry-infused gin in a cocktail shaker. Add ice and shake vigorously to chill, then strain into an old-fashioned glass filled with crushed ice. Garnish with a basil leaf and lime zest.

GRILLED POLENTA

The final brushing of lemon juice, olive oil, and salt brightens up the polenta before grilling. This versatile side dish can also be topped with anything from a vegetable ragout to braised meats. Recipe courtesy of Executive Chef Sonya Coté.

SERVES 8–10

1¼ cups whole milk

1¼ cups water

Salt and white pepper to taste

1 cup yellow cornmeal

1½ tablespoons unsalted butter

¼ cup mascarpone cheese

¼ cup grated Parmesan cheese

1 tablespoon lemon juice

¼ cup olive oil

In a medium saucepan, bring the milk, water, salt, and white pepper to a low boil over medium heat. Slowly whisk in the cornmeal, then reduce heat to low and cook for 20 minutes, stirring occasionally.

When the polenta is tender, remove from heat and stir in butter, mascarpone, and Parmesan.

Line a 9 x 13-inch baking dish with parchment paper. Pour the polenta on to the parchment and spread into a smooth, even layer. Cut another piece of parchment paper the same size, and press it on top of the polenta, smoothing it out evenly. Refrigerate until the polenta is firm, at least 1 hour.

Preheat a grill to medium high.

Cut firm polenta into circles, triangles, or other desired shape.

In a small bowl, combine lemon juice, olive oil, and salt to taste. Brush this mixture on both sides of each polenta piece and grill to create sear marks on both sides.

To serve, drizzle the polenta with the remaining lemon/oil mixture. Serve hot.

The Backspace

507 San Jacinto Boulevard
Austin, TX 78701
(512) 474-9899
http://thebackspace-austin.com/
Restaurateur/Chef: Shawn Cirkiel

The Backspace is just that—a small restaurant space on the back side of Shawn Cirkiel's Parkside (page 172) downtown. This tiny jewel box feels like a bit of Italy mixed with a bit of New York—bustling, cozy, and home to some of the best pizza in Austin.

The centerpiece of the restaurant is the huge wood-fired oven that is the only cooking surface in the place. At temperatures of up to 1,000°F, it is the perfect vessel for baking chewy-crust pizzas and sizzling dishes of appetizers. The Neapolitan-style pizzas have beautifully bubbled crusts and simple but flavorful toppings. The marinara pizza is topped with a simple tomato sauce and sliced garlic, while the white anchovy pie comes studded with olives, cherry tomatoes, and a sprinkle of oregano. A whole egg or slices of prosciutto can be added on top of any pizza.

Many of the antipasti at Backspace are also cooked in the oak-fired oven. A dish of baked ricotta is dressed up with poached tomatoes, olive oil, and lemon, while a mix of Castelvetrano and Gaeta olives are served bubbling in an oil marinade with citrus and herbs. *Salumi* and cheese plates, along with fresh salads topped with giardiniera or fennel offer cool alternatives for starters. Just as tempting are the desserts, all miniature jars filled with light tiramisu, rich ricotta cheesecake, or the creamy hazelnut *budino.* The wine list is all Italian, and the only beer offered is Peroni on draft.

With so few tables and bar seats, the restaurant is a great option for couples or groups of four or less. While waiting for a table, many guests have a seat at the bar at next-door Parkside. The Backspace is a miniature haven of good food and drink in the middle of downtown's lively 6th Street district, and the excellent pizza is just one of many reasons to visit.

Giardiniera

At The Backspace, this bright and tangy mix of vegetables is served on salad greens with red onion, fresh herbs, and pecorino Romano cheese. The mix would also brighten up sandwiches or be great alone as a snack. Recipe courtesy of Chef Shawn Cirkiel.

MAKES ABOUT 1 QUART

1 cup chopped cauliflower
½ cup chopped celery
½ cup sliced carrot
¼ cup julienned red bell pepper
3 whole garlic cloves

¼ teaspoon mustard seed
¼ teaspoon fennel seed
1 bay leaf
¼ teaspoon peppercorns
1 small sprig fresh thyme

1 cup white wine vinegar

1 cup water

1½ teaspoons kosher salt

¾ teaspoon granulated sugar

Add the vegetables and garlic to a quart-size canning jar.

Combine the mustard seed, fennel seed, bay leaf, peppercorns, and thyme; tie up in a sachet made of cheesecloth and set aside.

Bring the vinegar, water, salt, sugar, and prepared spice sachet to a boil. Remove from the heat and pour over the vegetables in the jar; discard the spice sachet. Cover tightly and refrigerate until chilled. The mixture will keep for up to 1 week.

BUTTERNUT SQUASH WITH PUMPKIN SEED PESTO

At The Backspace, the butternut squash is baked in the oak-fired oven at extremely high temperatures. Chef Cirkiel has adjusted the recipe for home ovens. The recipe would work with any winter squash, and the pumpkin seed pesto would be just as delicious mixed with pasta or smeared on toasted baguette. Recipe courtesy of Chef Shawn Cirkiel.

SERVES 8–10

For the butternut squash:

3 whole butternut squash (about 2 pounds each),
    peeled, seeded, and cubed
¼ cup extra-virgin olive oil
Salt and pepper to taste

For the pumpkin seed pesto:

1 cup flat-leaf parsley
1 cup fresh basil
1 cup toasted pumpkin seeds
2 tablespoons chopped garlic
2 cups extra-virgin olive oil
3 tablespoons lemon juice
Salt and pepper to taste

Preheat oven to 400°F.

To prepare the butternut squash: Toss squash with olive oil. Season liberally with salt and pepper. Place on a large baking sheet in one layer, and bake for 45 minutes, or until butternut squash is fork tender and has begun to caramelize.

To prepare the pesto: Blanch the parsley and basil separately in boiling water. Shock in ice water and wring dry.

Combine the parsley, basil, pumpkin seeds, and garlic in a blender. Puree, and slowly stream in the olive oil and lemon juice with the blender running. When fully blended and emulsified, season with salt and pepper to taste.

Top the roasted squash with a dollop of pesto and serve immediately.

COCKTAIL CULTURE

Just a few years ago, the cocktail scene in Austin was one of vodka-and-sodas at downtown bars and frozen margaritas at Tex-Mex restaurants. Now, well-crafted cocktails can be found all over the city.

Bartenders have for the most part embraced the craft cocktail movement, bringing back classic drinks, updating old recipes, and creating new mixes. Menus range from classics like daiquiris and old-fashioneds to spirit-heavy drinks meant for sipping slowly. With an emphasis on fresh juices and herbs, house-made bitters, and carefully chosen forms of ice, the craft cocktail is meticulously measured, expertly prepared, and perfectly balanced.

While there are several cocktail bars in Austin, such as the Tigress Pub and Drink, there are also plenty of restaurants whose cocktail programs are just as important as their food menus. From FINO (page 46) and East Side Showroom (page 118) to Contigo (page 57) and La Condesa (page 116), these eateries have employed some of the best bartenders to create their bar menus. An exciting addition to Austin's cocktail scene is the Midnight Cowboy (www.midnightcowboymodeling.com), a reservation-only spot where guests receive craft cocktails prepared tableside.

With all of these new cocktail options, Austin still loves the margarita, the Mexican martini, and the *michelada*. There is room for it all in a city as diverse and creative as Austin.

Jack Allen's Kitchen

7720 TX 71 West
Austin, TX 78735
(512) 852-8558
WWW.JACKALLENSKITCHEN.COM
Owner/Chef: Jack Gilmore

Jack Allen's Kitchen is 6,500 square feet of pure Texas hospitality. Chef and owner Jack Gilmore has created an upscale-casual space with dishes inspired by local produce and meats. He visits several farmers' markets a week to find the freshest ingredients, then transforms them into savory dishes with a definite Southwestern feel. Diners are greeted at the table with a complimentary dish of house-made pimiento cheese and flatbread crackers, and the friendliness and flavor extend from there.

The menu ranges from bacon-wrapped Texas quail to green chile pork tacos. Chicken-fried beef ribs are served alongside creamy blue-crab gratin. Meats, which are generally locally sourced, are most often grilled or seared, country fried, or cooked with spicy chiles. Salads feature locally grown produce, and cocktails are made with fresh juices and herbs. Sunday brunch is a buffet affair, with enticing dishes such as jalapeño sausage, house-cured ham, and green chile pork and eggs.

The space itself is modern and welcoming. Chef Gilmore and his team have worked hard to turn a large, industrial building into a warm and inviting space with reclaimed barn wood and a lively patio bar. The restaurant easily seats 350 guests. Serving consistently great food and cocktails with a local focus to that many people is no easy feat, but Jack Allen's does it with a smile.

Chef Gilmore is passionate about giving back to his community. He hosts fund-raising events for the likes of the Lonestar Paralysis Foundation and has raised money for those affected in 2011's Texas wildfires. Thanksgiving often sees Chef Gilmore serving a feast to public servants and their families—military servicemen and servicewomen, firefighters, and the like. The restaurant's devotion to great service and hospitality is just an extension of Chef Gilmore's own generosity and commitment to his community.

Tamale & Jalapeño Corn Bread Dressing

A staple on Chef Gilmore's charity Thanksgiving menus is this moist and flavorful dressing. Studded with jalapeños and chunks of tamales, it definitely has a Southwestern flair. The sweet corn and red bell peppers add a touch of sweetness to the dish. Recipe courtesy of Chef Jack Gilmore.

SERVES 12–15

6 tablespoons (¾ stick) butter, divided
1½ cups chopped onion
1½ cups chopped red bell pepper
2 cups chopped poblano peppers

3 large jalapeños, stemmed, seeded, and chopped
1 tablespoon chopped fresh sage or
    4 teaspoons dried sage
1½ tablespoons dried oregano

1½ pounds corn bread (use your favorite recipe)

¾ cup chopped fresh cilantro

1½ cups crushed corn chips

1½ cups frozen corn kernels, thawed

1¼ cups canned cream-style corn

2–3 cups chicken stock, heated

1 dozen tamales (use your favorite type),
 shucked and chopped into 1-inch pieces

Salt and pepper to taste

In a large, heavy skillet, melt 4 tablespoons butter over medium heat. Add the onion, bell pepper, poblano peppers, jalapeños, sage, and oregano. Sauté until all vegetables are tender.

Crumble the corn bread in a large bowl. Add the sautéed vegetables, cilantro, corn chips, kernel corn, cream-style corn, and 2 cups warm chicken stock, and mix thoroughly. Gently fold in the tamales, being careful not to break them up. Finally, season with salt and pepper to taste. If the stuffing feels too dry, add a little melted butter or more stock.

Preheat the oven to 325°F. Use the remaining 2 tablespoons butter to coat a 9 x 13-inch baking dish.

Pour the cornbread mixture into the baking dish and cover with foil. Bake for about 45 minutes. Remove the foil and bake for another 15 minutes, or until the stuffing has browned slightly.

Perfect Pairing

TITO'S SAGE GRAPEFRUIT SPLASH

The cocktails at Jack Allen's Kitchen feature fresh juices and herbs mixed with local spirits, like this bright and delicious drink. You can substitute your favorite vodka if you can't find Tito's. Recipe courtesy of Chef Jack Gilmore.

SERVES 1

4 fresh sage leaves

¾ ounce simple syrup (page 24)

Ice

1½ ounces Tito's vodka

¾ ounce St-Germain elderflower liqueur

2 ounces freshly squeezed grapefruit juice

Lemon wedge

Soda water

In a mixing glass, muddle sage with simple syrup. Fill the glass with ice, then add vodka, elderflower liqueur, grapefruit juice, and the juice of the lemon wedge. Shake until chilled, then pour cocktail with ice into a margarita glass. Top with soda water to fill glass.

Casa de Luz

1701 Toomey Road
Austin, TX 78704
(512) 476-2535
www.casadeluz.org
Nonprofit Organization

First and foremost, Casa de Luz is not a typical restaurant. It was established as a nonprofit organization in 1991, a continuation of the East-West Center that was started in 1985. Its mission is to bring health to the community by providing spaces for health-promoting activities such as yoga classes and meditation, as well as a nurturing dining room that serves vegan and organic meals daily.

Eduardo Longoria was integral in creating Casa de Luz, and he still remains involved in all processes. He believes that one of the most intimate relationships humans share is with their food, and that each meal should be taken with care. A sign above the cooking area reads, NATURE IS OUR MEAL PLANNER, and in accordance with this statement, each day's menu is chosen with respect for the organic produce that is available and seasonal.

The dining room is serene and calming, with communal tables, a relaxing patio, and a surprisingly quiet open kitchen. There is no menu—guests are served portions of whatever dishes have been created that day. Lunch or dinner might consist of a sweet potato–ginger soup, salad with house-made dressing, beans, grains, cooked greens, steamed squash, and pickled cabbage. Tacos and chilaquiles made with fresh corn tortillas are favorites, as well as any of the well-seasoned sauces, condiments, and dressings. Breakfasts feature cooked whole grains and fresh fruit as well as a variety of beans and vegetables. Everything is prepared simply with minimal processing, which helps to highlight the flavors of the vegetables, beans, and grains.

Guests can choose to enjoy a nourishing meal alone or to join others for friendly conversation at community tables. Either way, a meal taken at Casa de Luz nourishes both the body and the mind.

Butternut Squash Millet with Tahini Parsley Sauce

This recipe is a good representation of the type of food served at Casa de Luz. Healthy whole grains are paired with vegetables and simply dressed with a flavorful sauce. At Casa de Luz, this would likely be served with steamed vegetables, blanched greens, beans, soup, and salad. At home, this could easily be served as an entree or a side dish, and it's a great way to introduce whole grains to a meal. Recipe courtesy of Casa de Luz.

SERVES 8–10

For the butternut squash millet:

2 cups millet
2 cups 1-inch cubes of butternut squash
6 cups water
Pinch of salt

For the tahini parsley sauce:

1 cup lightly roasted sesame seeds
    (or ½ cup prepared tahini)
1 tablespoon lemon juice
1 cup warm water
1 clove garlic
2 tablespoons finely chopped parsley
Salt and pepper to taste

Toasted sunflower seeds, for serving

To prepare the millet: Rinse the millet and drain. In a large saucepan, bring millet, butternut squash, water, and salt to a boil. Reduce heat to low and simmer, covered, until water is absorbed, about 40 minutes. Stir well to blend ingredients.

To prepare the tahini parsley sauce: Combine all ingredients in a blender and puree for 1 minute, or until smooth.

To serve: Scoop millet mixture onto a plate, top with sauce, and sprinkle with sunflower seeds.

IMPERIA

310 COLORADO STREET
AUSTIN, TX 78701
(512) 472-6770
HTTP://IMPERIA-AUSTIN.COM
CO-OWNERS: MICHAEL L. GIRARD AND DIGGY TAYLOR

A swank and modern space in the heart of the warehouse district in downtown Austin, Imperia serves Asian fusion cuisine along with excellent sushi and nigiri. The interior feels posh and urban, with red and black accents and sleek surfaces. Guests can choose to sit in the dining room or lounge area as well as at the sushi bar.

The restaurant becomes a hot spot on weekend evenings, when pretty young things hang out at the bar sipping martinis and snacking on edamame. Still, the dining room is a surprisingly great spot to try out creative sushi rolls and entrees. There are plenty of small plates for sharing, including the popular house spicy edamame, the tender sea bass *kushiyaki* skewers, and the sugarcane duck kebabs. Larger plates include pan-fried noodles with beef and shishito peppers, a Thai tofu clay pot with coconut curry, and Peking duck for two.

The nigiri and sashimi at Imperia are freshly sliced, and the rolls are inventive and fresh. From the Bank Roll, made with *unagi* and cream cheese, to the sashimi platter, the ingredients are of top quality and are creatively combined. The *omakase* menu allows the chef to prepare what is freshest and seasonal for diners, and is available at the three- and five-course level.

The beverage menu has plenty of wines by the glass and specialty cocktails, which keep diners in the lounge area for hours after dinner. Always a place to see and be seen, Imperia is also a little-known spot for great sushi and fusion dishes.

SPICY EDAMAME

A popular menu item, this dish takes steamed edamame to the next level, adding the spiciness of chiles and the brightness of citrus. You can use a large skillet, but you may have to cook the edamame in two batches. The pods should spread out in one layer to allow them to char rather than steam. Recipe courtesy of Imperia.

SERVES 4

1 tablespoon peanut oil
1–2 Fresno chiles, sliced
1 pound cooked edamame pods
1 tablespoon lemon zest
1½ teaspoons sea salt
1 tablespoon lemon juice
½ teaspoon sea salt flakes, for garnish

Add the oil to a hot wok over high heat. Add the chiles and sauté for 30 seconds. Add the edamame and cook, stirring, until the pods begin to char. Add the lemon zest and toss to coat. Spread the pods out in one layer in the wok and allow to char a bit more. Season with 1½ teaspoons salt and toss to coat. Spread the pods out once more and allow them to char again. Remove from the heat and add the lemon juice; toss to coat. Garnish with sea salt flakes and serve.

Perfect Pairing

YIN YANG CHOCOLATE MARTINI

A dessert in a glass, this martini swirls together cream and chocolate for a decadent and sweet end to a meal. Recipe courtesy of Imperia.

SERVES 1

1 teaspoon chocolate sauce
1¼ ounces whipped cream–flavored vodka
    (such as Pinnacle)
1 ounce chocolate liqueur (such as Trader Vic's)
Splash of half-and-half
Ice
Cocoa powder, for dusting

Swirl chocolate sauce in the bottom and on the sides of a chilled martini glass.

In a shaker, combine the vodka, chocolate liqueur, and half-and-half. Add ice and shake well. Strain into the prepared martini glass, and top with a light dusting of cocoa powder.

The Salt Lick

18300 Farm to Market Road 1826
Driftwood, TX 78619
(512) 858-4959
www.saltlickbbq.com
Owner: Scott Roberts

Just a short drive away from Austin, The Salt Lick has been serving some of the area's favorite barbecue since 1967. With recipes handed down from generation to generation, owner Scott Roberts has maintained his family's legacy while cooking up barbecue that brings Austinites out to Driftwood on a regular basis.

The history of The Salt Lick dates back to the mid-1800s, when Roberts's family traveled by wagon from Mississippi to Texas. Along the way, the barbecue technique was perfected and handed down, eventually morphing into the very Texas-style method and flavor that is served today.

The Salt Lick sits among century-old oak trees and wildflowers and is a popular wedding and event location. The restaurant is centered around a huge open pit, where meats are seared and smoked. Over the years, the restaurant has grown to seat about eight hundred diners at once, and on any given weekend, diners may expect to wait a bit for a table. Meals can be served by the plate or family style, with all-you-can-eat brisket, sausage, ribs, and sides.

The Salt Lick creates their tender brisket and ribs by first searing them to lock in the juices, then slow cooking them over the coals. Diners can choose from pork or beef ribs, turkey, and the usual sausage and brisket. Only three sides are offered—coleslaw, pinto beans, and potato salad—and they are traditional and tasty versions that complement the barbecue well. Of course, sliced white bread, pickles, and onions are also available. Most guests don't leave without a bit of blackberry or peach cobbler with ice cream, the perfect ending to a Salt Lick meal.

The Salt Lick now has a second location north of Austin in Round Rock, but most Austinites choose to take a weekend drive south to enjoy the bluebonnets and other wildflowers along the way. The superb barbecue waiting at the end of the trip makes it all worthwhile.

SALT LICK PINTO BEANS

This recipe is a tribute to the beans that were originally cooked over wood fires on wagon trains. The pork adds a hint of meatiness and depth, while the butter rounds out the flavor of the pinto beans. The beans taste even better the second day, when the flavors have had time to meld. Recipe courtesy of The Salt Lick.

SERVES 4–6

8 cups water

1 pound dried pinto beans

2 ounces pork butt

¼ cup pinto bean seasoning, such as Fiesta brand

4 tablespoons unsalted butter

Add water to a large dutch oven (preferably cast iron) over medium-high heat.

While water is warming, clean and wash the dried beans. Place small amounts of beans on a baking sheet and sort through them to remove any shriveled beans or debris. Once cleaned, place the beans in a colander and run under cold water, swirling the beans with your hand.

Add beans to the dutch oven along with the pork. Bring the mixture to a rolling boil. Allow the beans to boil for 20 minutes, then reduce the heat to medium. Stir beans well, and add the bean spice. Stir well to incorporate the spice mixture.

Cook the beans at a simmer for 1–1½ hours, until the beans are tender, stirring occasionally.

Add the butter and stir well until thoroughly melted into the beans. Serve the beans hot.

THAI FRESH

909B WEST MARY STREET
AUSTIN, TX 78704
(512) 494-6436
HTTP://THAI-FRESH.COM/
CO-OWNERS: JAM SANITCHAT AND BRUCE BARNES

Before opening Thai Fresh, co-owner Jam Sanitchat taught cooking classes out of her home and sold her Thai dishes made from family recipes at local farmers' markets. As demand for her cooking and knowledge grew, she and her husband Bruce Barnes realized she needed her own restaurant kitchen to meet her needs.

Thai Fresh is many things—a Thai deli, a market, a cooking school, and a cultural center. Sanitchat wanted to cultivate a space where people could learn more about the Thai culture and taste authentic Thai dishes. Also important to her was sustainability— she has chosen to procure all of her meats from Texas producers who use no antibiotics or hormones. She uses as much local produce as possible, and has a strong connection to the Austin food and farm community.

The food at Thai Fresh is served deli style. It is prepared in small batches throughout the day, and diners can opt to take their dishes home or dine in the airy cafe. Satays and papaya salads, curries and pad thai all rotate through the display cases, and the staff can guide diners through flavors and combinations that work well together. Also available are freshly made ice creams, Thai tea, and specials featuring herbs and produce that are at their peak.

Thai Fresh also offers cooking classes three to four times a week. The classes focus on popular Thai dishes, vegetarian dishes, and street foods. The small classes (only fourteen students are allowed per class) mean that each participant has plenty of opportunities to get involved and ask questions. Many students return for subsequent classes, or to repeat classes that may feature new dishes. At the end of the class, many of the specialty ingredients can be purchased right there in the shop.

In 2011, Sanitchat and Barnes opened Thrice Cafe next door, a coffee shop with Thai-inspired snacks, live music, and beer and wine. Between the two locations, the couple has created a community space where visitors can dine on, learn about, and discuss Thai food and culture.

Kluay Khaek

FRIED BANANAS

As Thai meals are centered around rice, a variety of dishes, including these fried treats, make up the rest of the meal. While Sanitchat considers the fried bananas a side dish or small plate, the sweet bananas and coconut make this a great dessert option as well. Recipe courtesy of Jam Sanitchat.

SERVES 10

½ cup dried or frozen unsweetened, shredded coconut
¾ cup rice flour
¼ cup tapioca flour
¼ cup white sesame seeds
1 teaspoon salt
2 tablespoons sugar
¾–1 cup water
Vegetable oil, for frying
10 bananas, ripe but still firm, peeled

Combine the coconut, flours, sesame seeds, salt, and sugar in a medium bowl. Stir in enough water to make a pancake-batter consistency. Set aside.

Heat 2 inches of oil in a deep pan or deep fryer to 350°F.

Slice the bananas in half lengthwise, then into 2 or 3 pieces widthwise. Dip the banana pieces in the batter one at a time, and make sure each piece is coated in batter. Fry in hot oil in small batches until golden brown. Drain on paper towels.

Nam Prik Ong

NORTHERN PORK & TOMATO RELISH

This meaty dip starts with a spicy chile and tomato paste that is then cooked with minced pork. Traditionally, the dip is served with fresh vegetables and crispy pork skins as a component of a Thai meal. Recipe courtesy of Jam Sanitchat.

SERVES 3–4

For the paste:

5 dried long red Thai chiles, soaked for an hour
   in hot water, drained, and deseeded
Large pinch of salt
1 tablespoon chopped fresh lemongrass
3 tablespoons chopped shallot
2 tablespoons chopped garlic
1 teaspoon shrimp paste
1 cup coarsely chopped tomatoes

For the relish:

2 garlic cloves, peeled
Pinch of salt
3 tablespoons lard (or vegetable oil)
5 ounces minced pork
2 tablespoons fish sauce
Pinch of palm sugar
2 teaspoons vegetable stock

For serving:

Raw vegetables (cucumber, carrots, celery, radishes,
   turnips, etc.)
Steamed vegetables (green beans, Asian eggplant,
   cabbage, broccoli, cauliflower, etc.)
Crispy pork rinds

To prepare the paste: Pound the chiles with a mortar and pestle. Add the salt and pound again. Continue with each ingredient in order, until all ingredients have been pounded together to make a paste. Set aside.

To prepare the relish: Pound the garlic and salt together with a mortar and pestle.

Add lard or oil to a skillet over medium heat. Add garlic puree and sauté until fragrant and starting to brown, about 30 seconds. Add the prepared paste and continue to cook for several minutes, stirring constantly. Add the minced pork and stir to break up the meat. When pork is cooked through, season with fish sauce and palm sugar. If the mixture seems dry, add stock as needed.

To serve: Serve with raw and steamed vegetables and crispy pork rinds.

CHEZ ZEE

5406 BALCONES DRIVE
AUSTIN, TX 78731
(512) 454-2666
WWW.CHEZ-ZEE.COM
OWNER: SHARON WATKINS

Since 1989, Austinites have shared anniversaries, birthdays, and engagements at Chez Zee. There is just something about the arched walkway of twinkle lights and the beautiful patio that invites people to celebrate.

Owner Sharon Watkins wanted to create a restaurant that was focused on the people who dined there. Her personality shines through in the rotating artwork, the strings of lights, the holiday decorations, and the board games on the patio. A red piano sits in the dining room, ready for musicians to tickle its keys every weekend evening. Watkins believes that her restaurant is about what people do when they come together, to eat, to talk, and to commemorate occasions. The beautiful bar, the low lighting, and the unobtrusive service create a romantic and elegant ambience that diners appreciate.

The menu at Chez Zee is large and varied, encompassing lunch, dinner, brunch, desserts, grill items, and even gluten-free dishes. Some dishes have been on the menu, in one iteration or another, since the restaurant opened, simply because regulars can't stand to lose them. Watkins keeps it fresh with seasonal specials and updates, which bring in new diners and regulars alike. A few long-time favorites of diners are the pecan-crusted chicken, served as a main dish or atop a salad, the Aztec corn and shrimp bisque, and the chicken Gorgonzola pizza. Chez Zee's signature crème brûlée french toast is divine, and the brunch menu also features a variety of Benedicts, omelets, and quiches.

Perhaps the most popular dishes at Chez Zee are the desserts. With an in-house bakery, the restaurant offers made-from-scratch specialties like their lemon rosemary cake, Coco Leches Cake, and Kahlúa crunch pie. With brownies and puddings, cheesecakes and tortes, the dessert menu is always tempting and exciting.

Watkins has strived to maintain the cozy atmosphere and excellent food at Chez Zee while focusing on sourcing the best ingredients and handling food with the utmost care. The food is made in small batches using real ingredients, and decorations and lights change seasonally. Locals visit for brunch gatherings, anniversary dinners, and first dates, and Chez Zee easily pleases them all.

SWEET POTATO PUDDING

This sweet and creamy side dish is a favorite of diners at Chez Zee. Shredding the sweet potatoes gives the finished dish an interesting texture. While this dish would be excellent for a holiday meal, it is so delicious that it would be welcome at any time of year.

SERVES 4–6

1 pound sweet potatoes, peeled and shredded on a large-hole grater (or in food processor with shredding attachment)
1 cup packed brown sugar
¾ teaspoon salt
2 teaspoons ground ginger
2 tablespoons cornmeal
1 egg
2 egg yolks
1 cup heavy cream
1 tablespoon vanilla extract

Preheat the oven to 275°F. Place a baking pan full of water on the bottom rack to create steam.

In a large mixing bowl, combine sweet potatoes, brown sugar, salt, ginger, and cornmeal. Mix thoroughly.

In a separate bowl, whisk together the egg, egg yolks, cream, and vanilla. Add to the sweet potato mixture and mix well. Pour the mixture into a greased 8 x 8-inch baking dish.

Bake the pudding on the top rack of the oven, over the steaming pan of water, for 45 minutes. Serve hot.

SHARON'S COLESLAW

A variation on the classic coleslaw, this version includes sweet red apples and carrots to add color and flavor. The lemon zest brightens up the simple dressing.

SERVES 8

For the dressing:

½ cup mayonnaise
1 tablespoon plus 1 teaspoon sugar
3 tablespoons minced yellow onion
1½ teaspoons lemon zest
3 tablespoons lemon juice
¼ teaspoon salt, or to taste
¼ teaspoon black pepper

For the coleslaw:

2 red apples, cored and shredded with a large-hole grater
8 cups shredded green cabbage (about 2 pounds)
2 carrots, shredded with a large-hole grater

To prepare the dressing: Combine all ingredients in a medium-size bowl and whisk until thoroughly combined. Set aside.

To prepare the coleslaw: Combine all ingredients with ⅔ cup of the prepared dressing, and toss until the vegetables are well coated.

Recipes courtesy of Sharon Watkins.

BRUNCH

For many people, brunch is that lazy meal of the week, when the Sunday paper is enjoyed over coffee and pancakes. For others, it's the perfect time to catch up with friends after a busy weekend while drinking mimosas and enjoying an array of breakfast and lunch items. In any case, brunch is a bit more laid-back, more relaxed than other meals of the week.

Austin loves brunch. With many late weekend nights spent enjoying live music and cocktails, a late morning meal is much appreciated. Several local restaurants serve Sunday brunch, which is often the most popular meal of the week.

For lighter and healthier brunch options, look to JuiceLand's Originator (page 151) or Orange Kush (page 151), or try Kerbey Lane's Tofu Scramble (page 160). Or splurge on a plate of Southern Hoecakes from Olivia (page 167), Drunken Doughnuts from Trace (page 161), or Foreign & Domestic's Fried Chicken Biscuit with Redeye Gravy, Romaine Slaw & Lemon Jam (page 145).

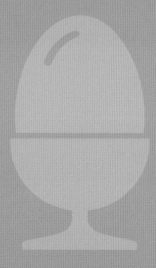

Foreign & Domestic Food & Drink

306 East 53rd Street
Austin, TX 78751
(512) 459-1010
http://fndaustin.com/
Co-owner/Executive Chef: Ned Elliott
Co-owner/Pastry Chef: Jodi Elliott

After cooking and baking their way through top restaurants in New York, London, and Portland, Oregon, Ned and Jodi Elliott headed to Austin to open a restaurant of their own. Foreign & Domestic was opened in May of 2010, and since then, Ned's savory creations and Jodi's decadent desserts have wowed Austinites and national audiences alike.

Ned and Jodi wanted to create a neighborhood restaurant, where local diners could expect excellent food and great service. It is not easy to define the food at Foreign & Domestic—the dishes often introduce diners to new ingredients in a playful way, while still remaining approachable to the average diner. The menu includes uncommon dishes like pigs' brains and huckleberries or beef heart tartare, but it is equally balanced with comforting choices like a chanterelle mushroom soup or duck fat–fried chicken.

Jodi's desserts are equally clever, with layers of flavor, texture, and temperature. The banana tart is made with a sandwich of pecan shortbread and caramelized banana custard, placed in a deep bowl and topped with caramel whipped cream, mocha ice, and spiced maple pecans. Fruit strudels are served with ginger ice cream, and basil snow cones are as welcome as chocolate-nut tarts. Jodi creates fun sweets that beg for diners to dig in and enjoy.

The restaurant no longer serves Sunday brunch, but in-the-know diners line up early for their occasional Saturday bake sales, featuring Jodi's breakfast pastries, desserts, and her famous Gruyere and Black Pepper Popovers. Surprisingly, with all of these inspired dishes and exciting ingredients, with excellent wine choices and multiple courses, the pricing is still affordable, and the experience is still approachable. With any visit to Foreign & Domestic, diners can expect a wonderful meal, whether they branch out to try new things or stick with updated classics.

Fried Chicken & Biscuit with Redeye Gravy, Romaine Slaw & Lemon Jam

The fried chicken biscuit is one of the most popular items on Foreign & Domestic's menu. The chicken is fried in duck fat, then served with a cheddar biscuit, redeye gravy, a crunchy romaine slaw, and lemon marmalade. Recipe courtesy of Executive Chef Ned Elliott.

SERVES 4

For the fried chicken:

3 cups buttermilk
½ teaspoon paprika
½ teaspoon black pepper
½ teaspoon onion powder
½ teaspoon garlic powder
4 boneless, skinless chicken thighs
Canola oil, for frying
2 cups all-purpose flour
½ teaspoon smoked paprika
1 teaspoon salt
1 tablespoon black pepper

For the lemon jam:

3 lemons, cut into thin rounds, seeds removed
1½ cups water
1½ cups sugar

For the cheddar biscuits:

3 ½ cups all-purpose flour, plus more for rolling out
2 tablespoons plus 1 teaspoon baking powder
¼ teaspoon baking soda
1 tablespoon sugar
1½ teaspoons salt
1½ teaspoons ground black pepper
4 ounces (about ½ cup plus 1½ tablespoons) cold shortening, cubed
¼ cup (½ stick) cold butter, cubed, plus more for brushing
1 cup shredded medium cheddar cheese
1½ cups buttermilk

For the redeye gravy:

½ cup butter
¾ cup all-purpose flour
3 tablespoons ground espresso beans
3 tablespoons brewed espresso
2 cups cooked spicy pork sausage, chopped
2 cups milk
2 cups heavy cream
1 tablespoon paprika
½ teaspoon garlic powder
2 tablespoons Tabasco sauce
Salt and pepper to taste

For the romaine slaw:

2 hearts of romaine, cut crosswise into ¼-inch strips
¼ cup sour cream
2 tablespoons olive oil
¼ cup chopped fresh chives
½ cup pickled red onions
¼ cup sliced pickled jalapeños
Salt and pepper to taste

4 fried eggs

Special equipment:

3-inch biscuit cutter

To prepare the fried chicken: Combine the buttermilk, paprika, pepper, onion powder, and garlic powder in a large bowl. Add the chicken thighs and marinate in the refrigerator for 24 hours.

To prepare the lemon jam: Place the lemon slices in a small saucepan and cover with water and sugar. Cook on low heat for about 2 hours, stirring occasionally, until the mixture has cooked down to a syrup-like consistency.

To prepare the cheddar biscuits: Preheat the oven to 350°F.

Combine flour, baking powder, baking soda, sugar, salt, and pepper in the bowl of a standing mixer fitted with the paddle attachment. Add shortening and butter and mix on low speed until mixture resembles cornmeal. Add cheese and mix. Slowly stir in buttermilk while mixing on low speed, just until combined; do not overmix.

Turn the dough out onto a lightly floured surface and roll out to about 1-inch thickness; be careful not to overwork the dough. Cut using a 3-inch biscuit cutter and place biscuits on a sheet pan lined with parchment paper. Brush with melted butter. Bake for 12–15 minutes, or until tops are just golden brown.

To prepare the redeye gravy: Make a roux by combining the butter and flour in a saucepan, and cook over medium heat, stirring frequently, for about 20 minutes. Add ground and brewed espresso, sausage, milk, and cream, and stir well to incorporate. Add paprika, garlic powder, Tabasco, and salt and pepper to taste. Cook on low heat for about 45 minutes, or until the mixture has a thick, gravy consistency.

To prepare the romaine slaw: Combine all ingredients in a large salad bowl and toss well.

To finish the fried chicken: Heat oil in a fryer or deep skillet to 320°F.

Combine the flour, smoked paprika, and salt and pepper to taste in a shallow bowl. Drain the thighs in a colander, then dredge in the flour mixture. Fry a few pieces at a time in the hot oil until the chicken reaches an internal temperature of 165°F and has a golden brown crust.

For each serving, place a dollop of redeye gravy in the center of the plate. Cut a biscuit in half and place the bottom half atop the gravy. Top with a fried chicken thigh, another dollop of gravy, a fried egg, ½ cup romaine slaw, and a dollop of lemon jam. Place the other half of the biscuit on top and drizzle with ½ cup more gravy.

Cottage Cheese Pancakes with Peach Jam

Jodi adapted this pancake recipe from Ned's mother. They are light and fluffy, and are wonderful when served with whipped crème fraîche and peach jam. Top with maple syrup for a sweet and special brunch. Recipe courtesy of Pastry Chef Jodi Elliott.

MAKES 3 SERVINGS

For the peach jam:

1 cup sugar

2 tablespoons water

2 pounds sliced peaches, fresh or frozen

½ cup white wine vinegar

½ teaspoon salt

¼ teaspoon ground cinnamon

¼ teaspoon ground nutmeg

¼ teaspoon ground coriander

1 teaspoon vanilla

For the whipped crème fraîche:

1 cup crème fraîche

3 tablespoons lemon juice

1¾ cups heavy whipping cream

1 cup confectioners' sugar

For the pancakes:

2 cups flour

3 teaspoons baking powder

4 teaspoons sugar

1 teaspoon salt

1 cup small-curd cottage cheese

1¾ cups milk

2 eggs, beaten

6 tablespoons (¾ stick) melted butter,
    plus more for the griddle

To prepare the peach jam: Add the sugar and water to a saucepan; the mixture should resemble wet sand. Heat over medium heat; do not stir. Allow the sugar to caramelize to a medium amber color. Carefully add remaining ingredients and stir together (be careful, as caramelized sugar may pop or splash when ingredients are added). Cook until the peaches break down and the mixture thickens, about 20–30 minutes, stirring occasionally. Let cool. The jam keeps for about 2 weeks, refrigerated, in a tightly sealed container.

To prepare the whipped crème fraîche: Combine all ingredients and whip with an electric mixer to stiff peaks. Whipped crème fraîche will start to deflate after a few hours, so prepare this just in advance of the pancakes.

To prepare the pancakes: Combine flour, baking powder, sugar, and salt in a large bowl. Make a well in the center.

Whisk together the cottage cheese, milk, and egg in a separate bowl; add all at once to dry ingredients and stir just until combined. Stir in melted butter; avoid overmixing.

Heat a griddle or nonstick skillet over medium heat. Butter the griddle as the cottage cheese may cause the pancakes to stick. Ladle ¾ cup batter on and allow it to spread a bit. Cook until bubbles form on the top side, then flip and cook until both sides are golden.

To serve: Stack 3 pancakes on each plate. Top with a dollop of crème fraîche and a dollop of peach jam.

JuiceLand

1625 Barton Springs Road
Austin, TX 78704
(512) 480-9501
http://juicelandaustin.com
Owner: Matt Shook

JuiceLand is authentically Austin. For the past decade, owner Matt Shook has worked to create a place where Austinites can go to feel good—both physically and spiritually. He sees JuiceLand as a wellness center of sorts, where people are encouraged to be themselves, to feed their bodies well, and to interact with their community.

The Barton Springs location is housed in the oldest building on the street and is surrounded with whimsical sculptures and creative outdoor seating. The building is covered with ephemera and statuettes, inside and out. Shook encourages his staff to be authentic in their decor, clothing, and even music choices at the shop. A visit to JuiceLand is invigorating, and not just because of the smoothies.

The menu boasts every type of fresh juice, smoothie, and cleanse you could imagine. From a simple apple-strawberry-banana smoothie to one with kale, hemp seeds, and spirulina, there is something for everyone. JuiceLand is an everyday place— customers often stop in once a day for their favorite energy booster, and visitors to Barton Springs pool often pop in for a hydrating juice.

The staff at JuiceLand are friendly and ready to help build the perfect juice or smoothie. If you're looking for an energy boost, they might steer you toward the Orange Kush, which is made with energizing yerba maté concentrate. For a protein boost with a jolt of vitamins, you might try a Wundershowzen, made with spinach, banana, hemp protein, peanut butter, and rice milk. There is no end to the combinations of healthy ingredients here, and with freshly squeezed juices, the drinks are guaranteed to be tasty.

Shook also owns and manages JuiceBox, which has an abbreviated menu and shares a space with Austin's own Soup Peddler. He aspires to be an involved member of the community, welcoming customers, participating at festivals, and providing Austinites with healthy food options. Whether customers are visiting for the first time, or are on day six of a juice cleanse, JuiceLand is a highlight of the day—funky, uplifting, and definitely delicious.

Originator

The Originator is JuiceLand's bestseller, and is chock-full of fruit and protein, making it a great brunch option. Recipe courtesy of Matt Shook.

MAKES 1 (16-OUNCE) SMOOTHIE

1 cup frozen banana pieces
½ cup frozen blueberries
¼ cup frozen pitted dark cherries
1½ cups freshly squeezed apple juice
1 tablespoon peanut butter
2 tablespoons egg white protein
1 teaspoon flaxseed oil
1 teaspoon spirulina

Add all ingredients to a blender and puree until smooth. Make sure it stays extra thick, adding the juice gradually depending on how solid the frozen fruit is.

Orange Kush

The Orange Kush features stimulating yerba maté and nutrient-packed hemp seeds, making it the perfect hangover smoothie. Recipe courtesy of Matt Shook.

MAKES 1 (16-OUNCE) SMOOTHIE

½ cup frozen banana pieces
1 cup freshly squeezed orange juice
½ cup yerba maté concentrate (such as Guayaki)
1 tablespoon hemp seeds
1 tablespoon hemp protein
1 teaspoon hemp oil
1 teaspoon chopped fresh ginger (optional)

Add all ingredients to a blender and puree until smooth. Make sure the smoothie stays extra thick, adding the juice gradually, depending on how solid the frozen fruit is.

Hyde Park Bar & Grill

4206 Duval Street
Austin, TX 78751
(512) 458-3168
http://hpbng.com/
Owner: Bick Brown

Hyde Park Bar & Grill is an Austin landmark that has been serving home-style food to locals since 1982. It is easy to find, thanks to the giant fork that is perched out front, which may pierce a set of longhorns, a red heart, or a huge flower, depending on the season. Over the years, the restaurant has become a cornerstone for the Hyde Park neighborhood, and has grown to include a second location in south Austin.

The original location is warm and comfortable, with a central bar and several smaller dining rooms lined with windows. Couples stop in for cozy dinners, families gather at large tables, and singles lounge at the bar enjoying beer, cocktails, or selections from the large wine list.

Owner Bick Brown's goal in opening Hyde Park Bar & Grill so many years ago hasn't changed—he strives to serve quality food in a welcoming atmosphere. The menu borrows from several different cuisines, with dishes like chicken quesadillas and Asian steamed dumplings. Most popular, however, are the American classics that Hyde Park does so well—chicken-fried steak, juicy burgers, and their famous battered french fries. The fries are so popular as a side dish and an appetizer that the restaurant processes over 200,000 pounds of potatoes a year.

Hyde Park Bar & Grill is a popular brunch destination as well. From the classic eggs Benedict to a plate of Tex-Mex huevos rancheros, the menu offers a range of sweet and savory breakfast dishes along with mimosas and Bloody Marys. Hyde Park Bar & Grill has served Austin for three decades, and the classic American dishes will no doubt keep diners happy for decades to come.

GRILLED SALMON BENEDICT
ON PARMESAN POLENTA

Aside from the classic eggs Benedict, Hyde Park Bar & Grill runs specials like this grilled salmon Benedict with Parmesan polenta, which would make a great addition to a special brunch at home. Recipe courtesy of Chef Martin Frannea.

SERVES 8

For the Parmesan polenta:

4 cups cold water

2 teaspoons kosher salt to taste, plus more as needed

1½ cups yellow cornmeal

½ cup (1 stick) cold butter, cubed

1 cup shredded Parmesan cheese

1 teaspoon ground black pepper

Oil, for frying

For the hollandaise sauce:

2½ cups clarified butter

5 egg yolks

½ cup cold water

¼ cup white wine

¼ cup lemon juice

4 shakes Tabasco sauce

¼ teaspoon Worcestershire sauce

Small pinch of cayenne pepper

½ teaspoon salt, plus more as needed

For the grilled salmon Benedict:

2 quarts water

½ cup lemon juice or white vinegar

¼ cup kosher salt, plus more as needed for seasoning

2 pounds wild or Atlantic salmon fillets, cut into
2-ounce portions

Vegetable oil, for brushing on the salmon

Pepper to taste

16 eggs

1 red bell pepper, finely diced (optional)

¼ cup chopped fresh basil (optional)

To prepare the Parmesan polenta: Preheat the oven to 350°F.

Place the cold water in an ovenproof medium saucepan. Add salt and taste; the water should taste like seawater. Add more salt if needed.

Place the water over high heat. Add the cornmeal gradually while the water is still cold, whisking to combine. Bring the mixture to a boil, whisking often to remove lumps. Reduce heat to low and stir continuously for 1 minute; remove from heat. Cover the pan with a tight-fitting ovenproof lid or aluminum foil, and place in preheated oven. Bake for 1 hour without stirring.

Remove the polenta from the oven. There should be some browned cornmeal on the side of the pan, but the texture should not be gritty.

With a stiff whisk, quickly stir in the butter, Parmesan, and black pepper until well blended. Carefully pour the polenta into an ungreased 5 x 9-inch baking pan. Quickly smooth the surface of the polenta; one way to do this is to cover the hot polenta with plastic wrap, and use a clean towel on the surface of the wrap to smooth it out, then remove plastic wrap. Cool the polenta, uncovered, in the refrigerator for 1 hour. Cut the polenta into triangles or other shape.

To prepare the hollandaise sauce: Fill a large saucepan with 3 inches of water and place it over high heat. When the water boils, reduce to medium heat and keep it at a simmer.

Heat the clarified butter in a small saucepan or in the microwave until it reaches 160°F, and keep it warm.

Add egg yolks, water, white wine, lemon juice, Tabasco sauce, Worcestershire sauce, cayenne, and salt to a 3–4-quart stainless steel bowl. Whisk vigorously for 30 seconds. Place the bowl atop the boiling water and heat until temperature reaches 140°F, whisking constantly. Remove from heat.

While whisking vigorously, very slowly add the heated clarified butter to the egg yolk mixture. The final sauce should be at about 150°F. If it is cooler than this, return it to the saucepan of boiling water and whisk until 150°F is reached. Taste and season with more salt if needed. Keep warm; the sauce will keep for up to an hour.

To prepare the grilled salmon Benedict: Heat the water, lemon juice, and ¼ cup salt in a large saucepan over high heat. Bring the water to a boil, then reduce heat to a low simmer.

Brush the salmon pieces with oil and season with salt and pepper. Sear on a hot grill to desired doneness, and keep warm.

Fry, sauté, or grill the polenta pieces. For each serving, arrange 2 pieces on the plate. Place a piece of grilled salmon atop each polenta piece.

For each serving, poach 2 eggs in the simmering water. Place atop each piece of salmon and top with hollandaise sauce. Sprinkle with bell pepper and basil, if desired.

Huevos Rancheros

Huevos rancheros are a classic Austin brunch dish, and Hyde Park Bar & Grill's version is excellent. The ranchero sauce, made with both dried and fresh chiles, has a nice depth of flavor. Recipe courtesy of Chef Martin Frannea.

SERVES 8

For the ranchero sauce (makes 4 cups):

4 dried ancho or Guajillo chiles, seeds and stems removed
½–1 cup warm water
1 tablespoon vegetable oil
½ cup diced yellow onion
1 teaspoon minced garlic
2 cups diced canned tomatoes, with juice
2 Roma tomatoes, diced
½ cup diced poblano peppers
½ teaspoon ground cumin
½ teaspoon ground black pepper
3 or 4 shakes Tabasco sauce
1 tablespoon tomato paste

1 teaspoon chile powder
Kosher salt to taste

For the huevos rancheros:

Oil, for frying
4 corn tortillas, cut into thin strips
8 corn tortillas, left whole
Kosher salt to taste
16 eggs
4 cups warmed black beans, homemade or canned
4 cups shredded Monterey Jack cheese
½ cup crumbled queso fresco (optional)
4 medium Haas avocados, pitted, halved, and sliced

PASSION FRUIT & RASPBERRY MIMOSA

This beautiful drink is an upgrade from the usual mimosa. The bright red raspberry puree contrasts beautifully with the orange passion fruit puree before the sparkling wine is stirred in. Recipe courtesy Chef Martin Frannea.

SERVES 1

1 ounce passion fruit puree
1 ounce raspberry puree
4 ounces sparkling wine

Combine passion fruit and raspberry purees in a champagne glass; top with sparkling wine and stir.

To prepare the ranchero sauce: Add the dried chiles to a blender with ½ cup warm water. Puree, adding more water as needed to reach a paste-like consistency.

In a medium saucepan, heat the vegetable oil over medium-high heat until it just begins to smoke. Add the onions and cook until just starting to brown. Add the garlic and cook for 30 seconds, stirring continuously to keep it from burning.

Add the remaining ingredients and stir; bring to a boil, then reduce heat to low and simmer for 20–30 minutes. Taste and season with salt as needed.

To prepare the huevos rancheros: Heat at least 1 inch oil in a skillet to 350°F. Fry the tortilla strips until they just begin to brown; remove from oil and drain on paper towels. Sprinkle with salt.

Fry the remaining whole tortillas, one at a time if needed to avoid crowding, until just beginning to brown. Remove from oil and drain on paper towels. Sprinkle with salt.

Reheat ranchero sauce if necessary. Cook 2 eggs per person as desired; fried eggs are preferred, but scrambled eggs also work.

For each serving, place a fried whole tortilla in the center of a plate. Surround the tortilla with ½ cup black beans. Spoon ½ cup ranchero sauce over the tortilla, then top with ½ cup shredded cheese. Top with 2 eggs, a few fried tortilla strips, and 1 tablespoon queso fresco, if desired. Finish with a few slices of avocado.

Kerbey Lane Cafe

3003 South Lamar Boulevard
Austin, TX 78704
(512) 445-4451
www.kerbeylanecafe.com
Owners: David Ayer and Patricia Atkinson

Kerbey Lane is one of Austin's oldest and most loved twenty-four-hour establishments. Since 1980, the restaurant has been an eccentric, laid-back favorite for diners of all types, at all hours. While the restaurant has expanded to five locations in Austin, each still feels personal, comfortable, and local.

The atmosphere at Kerbey Lane is casual and comfortable, and it definitely represents the local tagline of "keeping Austin weird." The walls display colorful works from local artists, and the staff represents all personalities and appearances. Management staff encourages employees to be themselves and let their personalities shine.

Always available on the menu are diner standbys like huge, fluffy pancakes, creamy queso, and hefty club sandwiches, but also of note is the seasonal menu, which changes throughout the year to highlight available produce and meats.

Kerbey Lane sources much of its produce and proteins locally, including all-natural meats, organic eggs, and vegetables from local farms. The summer menu is full of fresh tomato dishes, while the winter menu offers wild boar and bison chili Frito pie and stuffed acorn squash. There are plenty of vegetarian, vegan, and gluten-free options, making it easy for even the most diverse groups to share a great meal. Kerbey Lane strives to keep its menu fresh and relevant, and places a high priority on quality ingredients and food preparation.

While Austinites visit Kerbey Lane at all hours, weekend mornings are the busiest, as families line up to enjoy pancakes and omelets or burgers and fries. Whether you visit for brunch or for a 3 a.m. snack, you'll find that Kerbey Lane is consistently inviting, funky, and fun.

MIGAS

A flavorful mix of scrambled eggs, tortillas, chiles, and tomatoes, migas are the quintessential Austin breakfast dish (aside from the breakfast taco, of course). At Kerbey Lane Cafe, freshly made pico de gallo is cooked with the eggs and tortillas, and the whole thing is smothered in ranchero sauce. Migas recipe courtesy of David Ayer; ranchero sauce recipe courtesy of Patricia Atkinson.

SERVES 4

For the pico de gallo (makes about 4 cups):

3 tomatoes, seeded and diced
1 medium yellow onion, diced
2 jalapeños, seeded and diced
½ bunch cilantro, chopped
Juice of 1 lime
Kosher salt to taste

For the ranchero sauce (makes about 4 cups):

1 tablespoon canola oil
1 large yellow onion, diced
1 serrano pepper (or any fresh hot pepper), diced
4 cloves garlic
1 canned chipotle pepper, diced
1 teaspoon adobo sauce (from chipotle peppers)
½ teaspoon ground black pepper
2 teaspoons chile powder
2 (14.5-ounce) cans diced tomatoes
1 (6-ounce) can tomato sauce
Kosher salt to taste

For the migas:

2 tablespoons canola oil
8 eggs, beaten
1½ cups broken tortilla chips
1 cup grated cheese (a mixture of cheddar and
    Monterey Jack works well)
Warm tortillas, Spanish rice, and black beans,
    for serving (optional)

To prepare the pico de gallo: Combine all ingredients in a bowl. Season with salt to taste, and set aside. Pico de gallo will keep, refrigerated, for 1 day.

To prepare the ranchero sauce: Add the oil to a medium saucepan over medium heat. Add the onion and serrano pepper, and sauté until the onions are soft and translucent.

Add the onion mixture to a food processor bowl, along with the remaining ingredients. Pulse until well combined, but do not puree.

Transfer mixture back to the saucepan and simmer for about 30 minutes. Ranchero sauce will keep, refrigerated, for a week.

To prepare the migas: Add the oil to a large skillet over medium heat. Add 1 cup pico de gallo and sauté for about 1 minute. Add the eggs and stir gently. When the eggs are partially cooked, add the tortilla chips. Mix well until eggs are cooked to desired consistency.

Top with cheese and 1 cup warm ranchero sauce. (At Kerbey Lane the migas are served with warm tortillas, Spanish rice, and black beans.)

Tofu Scramble

Kerbey Lane Cafe has a wide variety of menu offerings for vegetarians and vegans. This dish is vegan but is full of flavor thanks to the fresh vegetables and herbs, spices, and cheese-like nutritional yeast. Recipe courtesy of Chef Joel Welch.

SERVES 2

1 pound firm tofu
3 tablespoons olive oil
1 tablespoon minced garlic
1 medium tomato, diced
1 jalapeño, seeded and diced
¼ cup diced onion
1 teaspoon chile powder
1 teaspoon salt
½ teaspoon black pepper
½ cup nutritional yeast
¼ bunch cilantro, chopped

Freeze tofu overnight; this improves its texture.

Thaw the tofu on a kitchen towel to soak up excess moisture. Once tofu is fully thawed, lightly squeeze it to remove any excess water. Break up the tofu into small chunks and set aside.

Add the oil to a large skillet over medium heat. Add the garlic, tomato, jalapeño, and onion, and sauté until the vegetables are softened. Add the chile powder, salt, and black pepper, and cook for 1 minute more. Stir in tofu, nutritional yeast, and cilantro. Cook until tofu is heated through.

TRACE RESTAURANT

200 LAVACA STREET
AUSTIN, TX 78701
(512) 542-3660
WWW.TRACEAUSTIN.COM

At the base of the posh W Austin Hotel, Trace Restaurant serves sophisticated food with a focus on sustainably and locally sourced ingredients. Employing a forager along with chef de cuisine and an executive pastry chef, the restaurant presents a thoughtful approach to menu creation.

The restaurant itself is sleek and sophisticated with plush gray banquettes and mosaic mirrors. The dark bar area opens up to the light dining area, and accents of orange break up the black, gray, and white. The seamless connection to the patio area makes the restaurant feel bright and airy. Many of the decorative items, and even the dining tables, were produced by local artisans and builders.

The menu encourages sharing among tablemates, with small plates and charcuterie boards. Onion rings, deviled eggs, and beet salads all feature local ingredients and fresh flavors. The charcuterie is made in-house, and the Market Snacks plate features produce and dishes that are seasonal and available that day. Dinner plates include crafted, foraged, and hunted ingredients such as handmade pastas, wild mushrooms, and venison with parsnips and black cherries. The restaurant also serves breakfast and weekend brunch, with buttermilk pancakes, omelets with market-fresh vegetables, and cinnamon-roll bread pudding.

The Trace team has created a refined menu that highlights the best that Austin's local growers, producers, and artisans have to offer. The restaurant's commitment to "conscious cuisine" shines through in every dish and is only enhanced by the fact that the food is beautifully presented and expertly prepared.

DRUNKEN DOUGHNUTS

These doughnuts, crispy on the outside and tender on the inside, are made even more decadent by the trio of boozy sauces for dipping. While dulce de leche can easily be purchased at Mexican markets, at Trace, it is made from scratch. Recipe courtesy of Executive Pastry Chef Janina O'Leary.

SERVES 4

For the bourbon dulce de leche:

1 (14-ounce) can sweetened condensed milk, unopened and dent-free
3 tablespoons bourbon

For the chile-tequila fudge sauce:

1 cup white sugar
3 tablespoons unsweetened cocoa powder
½ teaspoon salt
1 teaspoon ground cinnamon

¾ cup evaporated milk

1 teaspoon vanilla extract

2 tablespoons butter

2 tablespoons tequila

Pinch of cayenne pepper

For the vodka whipped cream:

1 quart whipping cream

2 tablespoons whipped-cream flavored vodka (such as
    Pinnacle)

For the doughnuts:

1½ cups milk

2½ ounces butter (about 1/3 cup)

2¼-ounce packages instant yeast

⅓ cup warm water (95°F–105°F)

2 eggs, beaten

¼ cup sugar

1½ teaspoons salt

1 teaspoon freshly grated nutmeg

4¾ cups all-purpose flour, plus more for rolling out
    dough

Vegetable oil, for frying (½–1 gallon, depending on fryer),
    plus more for oiling the bowl

Granulated sugar, for dusting

Special equipment:

2½-inch round biscuit cutter

To prepare the bourbon dulce de leche: Place the unopened can of sweetened condensed milk in a large pot and cover completely with water. Bring to a boil, then lower heat and simmer for 6 hours, adding more water as needed to always keep the can fully submerged. Remove the pot from heat and let the can cool completely in the water. Remove the can from the water; carefully open the can and spoon the dulce de leche into a small bowl. Stir in the bourbon and set aside.

To prepare the chile-tequila fudge sauce: Combine the sugar, cocoa powder, salt, and cinnamon in a medium saucepan, stirring to eliminate lumps. Add the evaporated milk and bring to a boil over medium-high heat. Boil for 2 minutes; remove from heat and stir in the vanilla and butter. Add the tequila and a pinch of cayenne pepper, and stir well to combine. Set aside.

To prepare the vodka whipped cream: Whip the cream to medium peaks. Fold in the vodka and set aside. The cream will begin to deflate after about half an hour, so make this just before serving.

To prepare the doughnuts: Heat the milk and butter in a medium saucepan over medium heat just until the butter is melted. Remove from heat; let cool to lukewarm temperature and set aside.

In a small bowl, sprinkle the yeast over the warm water and let dissolve for 5 minutes. Pour the yeast mixture into the large bowl of a standing mixer and add the cooled milk and butter mixture. Add the eggs, ¼ cup sugar, salt, nutmeg, and half the flour. Using the paddle attachment, combine the ingredients on low speed until flour is incorporated. Increase speed to medium and beat until well combined. Add the remaining flour, combining at low speed at first, then increasing speed to medium and beating well.

Switch to the dough hook attachment of the standing mixer and beat the mixture at medium speed until the dough pulls away from the bowl and becomes smooth, about 3–4 minutes. Transfer the dough to a well-oiled bowl, cover, and let rise for 1 hour or until doubled in size.

On a well-floured surface, roll out dough to 3/8-inch thickness. Cut using a 2½-inch round biscuit cutter. Set on a floured baking sheet, cover lightly with a tea towel, and let rise for 30 minutes.

Preheat the oil in a deep fryer or dutch oven to 365°F. Gently place the doughnuts in the oil, three or four at a time. Cook for 1 minute, then flip doughnuts and cook for 1 minute more.

Transfer to a cooling rack placed in a baking pan; immediately dredge in granulated sugar. Serve 5 doughnuts on a plate with the 3 dipping sauces in shot glasses.

Lavaca Omelet

The restaurant makes its own brisket for this Texan-inspired omelet, but you can also purchase a precooked brisket from your favorite barbecue spot. The greens, avocado, and salsa add bright colors and flavors to the dish. Recipe courtesy of Executive Chef Nadine Thomas.

SERVES 1

For the beef brisket:

1⅓ cups paprika
1 cup plus 2 tablespoons packed brown sugar
6 tablespoons plus ½ teaspoon sea salt
¼ cup granulated onion
½ cup dried thyme
¼ cup chile powder
1 tablespoon plus 2 teaspoons ground mustard
2 cups canola oil
1 (12-pound) brisket

For the sauce:

8 garlic cloves, smashed
5 red onions, diced
4 dried chiles de árbol, chopped
1 cup brown sugar
2 cups apple cider vinegar
½ cup tomato paste
¾ cup whole-grain mustard
7 quarts strong veal or chicken stock

For the salsa:

5 Roma tomatoes, roughly chopped
1 yellow onion, roughly chopped
1 cup pickled jalapeño slices
1 bunch cilantro, roughly chopped
1½ (10-ounce) cans diced tomatoes with green chiles
Juice of 3 limes

For the omelet:

1 tablespoon clarified butter
2 tablespoons chopped tomato
2 tablespoons minced red onion
1 tablespoon minced fresh jalapeño
1 garlic clove, minced
3 eggs, beaten
Salt and pepper to taste
¼ cup chopped cilantro leaves
⅓ cup shredded cheese

For serving:

2 tablespoons olive oil
1 tablespoon lime juice
1½ cups mixed greens
2 tablespoons sour cream
½ avocado, sliced
½ cup crispy tortilla strips (about ½ tortilla, thinly sliced and fried)

Special equipment:

Smoker (optional)

To prepare the brisket: Mix first seven ingredients with the oil and rub all over the brisket. Cover and refrigerate for 24 hours.

Smoke the brisket in a smoker for 2½ hours at 200°F with the smoke temperature at 300°F. Finish in a 275°F oven for 3 hours more. Remove from heat and reserve 1 cup of the rendered fat. Thinly slice the brisket and set aside.

To prepare the sauce: Combine all ingredients with the 1 cup reserved brisket fat in a large saucepan. Bring to a boil, then reduce heat to low, and simmer for 1 hour.

Pour the sauce over the brisket. Roughly chop about ½ cup of brisket with sauce for each omelet; set aside.

To prepare the salsa: Combine all ingredients in a blender and process for 30–40 seconds.

To prepare the omelet: Melt the clarified butter in an omelet pan or medium skillet over medium heat. Add chopped brisket and sauté until meat is crispy. Add the tomatoes, onion, jalapeños, and garlic, and sauté for a minute more. Add eggs and allow them to spread around the pan to create a wide omelet. Season with salt and pepper; when omelet is almost cooked through, top with cilantro and cheese and fold over. Remove from heat.

Before serving, whisk together the olive oil and lime juice in a small bowl. Toss with the mixed greens and place them on the plate. Place the omelet next to the greens and top with sour cream, avocado, and crispy tortilla strips. Spoon salsa next to the omelet.

Olivia

2043 South Lamar Boulevard
Austin, TX 78704
(512) 804-2700
http://olivia-austin.com/
Owner/Chef: James Holmes

The beautiful, sleek, and airy architecture of Olivia only serves to highlight the impeccably prepared food created by Chef James Holmes. Sunlight pours in during brunch and the early evening hours, and at night, the restaurant becomes a destination for romantic dinners, celebrations, and casual snacks at the bar.

The dining room's white walls and green and wood accents reflect the pure and natural menu that Chef Holmes has designed. Produce is sourced locally, as well as from the restaurant's own garden. A focus on vegetables and herbs means that meat dishes are more than just the locally sourced protein—they are balanced and enhanced by the freshest produce available. Nearby farmers, ranchers, and artisans happily share their ingredients with Olivia, as they are always treated with the utmost respect and creativity.

Diners can choose to visit the bar for snacks and drinks, or to have a seat in the dining room for a full dinner. Meals range from a few shared small plates to the grand chef's tasting menu, and none will disappoint. Sweetbreads are served with pickled blueberries and spring garlic, while salmon is paired with spring vegetables: green beans, sugar snap peas, cucumbers, and baby artichokes. If you have the time and inclination, the chef's tasting menu is a wonderful ten-course tour of the menu, and waitstaff are well-trained to suggest wine pairings with each course.

Sunday brunch at Olivia is not to be missed. Aside from fresh versions of the usual omelets and french toast, Olivia shines with its pickled pig's ear sandwich, lamb tongue tacos, and pork belly muffin sandwich. It would be a sin not to order a plate of picnic-style fried chicken for the table—Chef Holmes's recipe is so well-loved that he opened Lucy's Fried Chicken off nearby South Congress Avenue to appease the many requests for daily fried chicken.

A meal at Olivia can be an upscale, multi-course affair just as easily as a casual brunch get-together or a few snacks at the bar. Any of these options will result in expertly prepared, locally sourced dishes that highlight the best that Austin and central Texas has to offer.

SOUTHERN HOECAKES

These fluffy cornmeal pancakes are made even more decadent with a dollop of honey butter and a crumble of walnut toffee. A drizzle of pure maple syrup would put this dish over the top. Recipe courtesy of Chef Melissa Phillips.

SERVES 4

For the walnut toffee crumble:

2 cups sugar
1 pound (4 sticks) unsalted butter, cut into cubes
½ cup chopped, toasted walnuts

For the honey butter:

8 ounces (2 sticks) unsalted butter, softened
¼ cup honey

For the hoecakes:

1¼ cups all-purpose flour
1¼ cups cake flour, sifted
1 cup yellow cornmeal
1 tablespoon plus 1½ teaspoons baking powder
1½ teaspoons baking soda
3 tablespoons sugar
1 teaspoon salt
3 eggs
2 cups buttermilk
¼ cup (½ stick) melted unsalted butter
2 tablespoons oil or unsalted butter

Special equipment:

Baking sheet lined with nonstick silicone baking mat

To prepare the walnut toffee crumble: Heat sugar and butter in a large saucepan over medium-high heat, stirring until combined. Bring mixture to a boil; keep at a low boil, stirring occasionally until it is caramel colored and a candy thermometer reads 300°F. Stir in walnuts and immediately spread on a silicone-mat-lined baking sheet to cool. Once completely cooled, break into large chunks and place in a ziplock bag. Beat toffee with a mallet to break up into small pieces.

To prepare the honey butter: Combine the butter and honey in a large bowl. Beat with an electric mixer at medium speed until well combined. Taste and add more honey if desired. Store in the refrigerator until ready to use.

To prepare the hoecakes: Combine the dry ingredients in a medium bowl and whisk to combine. In a separate large bowl, whisk together eggs and buttermilk. Slowly add dry ingredients and stir just until combined. Pour in the melted butter and stir to incorporate. Do not overmix; some small lumps are okay.

Heat the oil or butter in a large cast-iron skillet or griddle over medium heat. For each hoecake pour about ¼ cup batter onto the griddle, keeping cakes about 2 inches apart. Cook, flipping once, until golden on both sides and cooked through, about 4–5 minutes. Serve with honey butter and walnut toffee crumble.

Lamar "Mac Daddy" Muffin Sandwich

Not your average breakfast sandwich, this version is stuffed with miso-rubbed, braised, then fried pork belly, plus a sweet chile glaze and a perfectly fried egg. Start a few days in advance to give the pork belly plenty of time to marinate. Recipe courtesy of Chef Andrew Francisco.

SERVES 4

For the pork belly:

¼ cup miso paste

3 tablespoons water

1 pound skinless pork belly

1 yellow onion, chopped

1 carrot, chopped

3 stalks celery, chopped

For the sweet chile glaze:

1 cup light brown sugar

1 cup apple cider vinegar

1 tablespoon minced ginger

1 tablespoon minced garlic

¼ cup minced yellow onion

3 tablespoons sambal chile sauce

1 kaffir lime leaf or zest of 1 lime

To assemble the sandwiches:

3 tablespoons butter

8 large eggs, beaten

8 English muffins, split in half and toasted

Canola oil, for frying

Kosher salt to taste

1 cup cilantro leaves

1 cup thinly sliced green onions

1–2 teaspoons olive oil

To prepare the pork belly: Three days before serving, marinate the pork belly. In a small bowl, combine the miso paste with water and whisk to combine. Rub mixture on both sides of pork belly and place in a medium dutch oven or ovenproof and stove-safe pot. Cover and refrigerate overnight or up to 2 days.

Once the pork has marinated at least 24 hours, preheat the oven to 300°F.

Add the onion, carrot, and celery to the pork belly and cover all with water. Place the dutch oven on the stovetop and bring liquid to a boil over high heat. Immediately remove from the heat and place in the oven. Bake for 1 ½–2 hours, or until pork is fork tender.

Remove the pork belly from the pot and place on a large baking sheet. Place another baking sheet on top and weigh it down (use cans or other heavy kitchen items) to press the pork belly. Refrigerate overnight.

To prepare the sweet chile glaze: Combine all ingredients in a medium saucepan and bring to a boil over high heat. Reduce heat to low and simmer, stirring to ensure sugar dissolves. Simmer until liquid is reduced by half, stirring occasionally. Let cool, and remove the lime leaf, if using.

To assemble the sandwiches: Melt the butter in a medium nonstick sauté pan over medium heat. Add eggs to the pan and scramble them to desired doneness. Divide evenly between 4 English muffin halves. In a deep sauté pan, heat about 1 inch canola oil to 350°F. Slice the pressed pork belly into 2-ounce pieces and fry in the oil until crispy on all sides. Remove from oil, sprinkle with kosher salt, then coat the pieces with the sweet chile glaze. Divide the pork evenly between the muffins, placing on top of the scrambled eggs.

In a small bowl, combine the cilantro leaves and green onions. Lightly dress with 1–2 teaspoons olive oil and sprinkle with kosher salt. Place the salad on top of the glazed pork belly, and top with the remaining 4 English muffin halves.

DESSERTS

Every meal (and cookbook) should end on a sweet note. Austin has a community of talented pastry chefs who create irresistible desserts, both traditional and extraordinary. While some restaurants boast a giant dessert menu with cakes, pies, sundaes and the like, others offer just a few expertly prepared delicacies. Treats can range from homey German chocolate cakes made from scratch and served with buttermilk ice cream to feats of molecular gastronomy with sweet foams, nitrogen-frozen ice creams, and delicate sheets of paper-thin chocolate or mango.

La Patisserie's Pistachio, Raspberry & Chocolate Cake (page 203) or the Chocolate Stout Cake from The Highball (page 189) would be fantastic and beautiful birthday desserts. The simple but lovely Tiramisu from ASTI Trattoria (page 197) or the zany "King Killer" Bark from Big Top Candy Shop (page 186) are perfect for new bakers, and the complex Banana Parfait with Cashew Ice Cream & Rum Caramel from Parkside (page 176) or Uchi's Coffee Panna Cotta with Mango Yolk (page 191) are challenging but worth the extra effort.

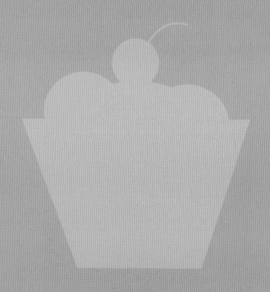

PARKSIDE

301 EAST 6TH STREET
AUSTIN, TX 78701
(512) 474-9898
HTTP://PARKSIDE-AUSTIN.COM/
RESTAURATEUR/CHEF: SHAWN CIRKIEL

In the heart of Austin's East 6th Street district downtown, Chef Shawn Cirkiel claimed one corner as his own and opened Parkside, a surprisingly sophisticated space in the middle of it all. Chef Cirkiel has always loved the energy of 6th Street, and though some critics worried about the feasibility of opening an upscale restaurant there, he has been able to pull it off with flair.

With two downstairs dining rooms, two bars, an upstairs patio, and a large event room, Parkside has become a downtown destination for every type of diner. Downstairs, the walls feature exposed brick and black-and-white photos from the chef's own family. Upstairs, the patio overlooks busy 6th Street and is ideal for people watching throughout the evening. Because of this always-lively view, Chef Cirkiel likes to think of Parkside as "the best dinner and a show on 6th street."

Parkside is perhaps most appealing because diners can opt for a raw oyster snack, an excellent burger and fries, or a multicourse plated dinner. One of the most coveted spots at Parkside is at the bar, where fresh oysters from Connecticut to British Columbia are shucked to order. Oyster platters and raw-bar treats like fluke with lemon and almonds or salmon with avocado and orange are beautifully prepared and served on ice. Shareable small plates include roasted marrow bones, crab fritters, and blond pâté with strawberry relish. Larger entrees such as locally sourced chicken and quail, seared scallops with couscous and olives, and green garlic risotto are creative and fresh. Pastry Chef Steven Cak has won diners over with his dessert menu. Roasted banana mousse is served with honey stout foam, while a passion fruit tart is paired with cashew crumble and mango sorbet.

Parkside continues to draw people to the 6th Street area who might not have headed there before. Chef Cirkiel's love for the city has helped to update the landscape and culture of East 6th Street in Austin, and his passion for creating great food can be appreciated in every dish at Parkside.

CHOCOLATE DOUGHNUTS WITH
PECAN BOURBON ICE CREAM & SQUASH CREAM

An elegant way to serve chocolate doughnuts, this dish features several components that can also be used on their own or with other desserts. The pecan bourbon ice cream and squash puree add a unique twist to the chocolate dessert. Recipe courtesy of Pastry Chef Steven Cak.

SERVES 8–10

For the pecan bourbon ice cream:

2 cups heavy cream
2 cups whole milk
1¼ cups sugar
2¼ cups pecans, toasted
12 egg yolks
2 tablespoons bourbon

For the spice blend:

2¾ teaspoons ground cinnamon
2½ teaspoons ground ginger
2 teaspoons ground nutmeg
1 teaspoon ground allspice

For the squash cream:

½ cup kabocha or butternut squash puree
¾ cup heavy cream
¾ cup whole milk
¾ cups plus 2 tablespoons sugar
⅓ gelatin sheet, bloomed in cold water
    for 3 to 5 minutes

For the chocolate paint:

1¼ cup water
¾ cup sugar
½ cup plus 1 tablespoon cocoa powder
3 ounces dark chocolate (at least 58%), chopped

For the pecan soil:

3 cups pecans
1 cup plus 2 tablespoons packed brown sugar
1⅓ cups all-purpose flour
2½ teaspoons salt
¾ cup (1½ sticks) unsalted butter, melted

For the chocolate doughnuts:

1¾ cups whole milk
1 tablespoon yeast
¼ cup plus 3 tablespoons sugar
1 large egg
2¾ cups bread flour
1½ cups plus 3 tablespoons cake flour
¾ cup plus 2 tablespoons Dutch-process cocoa powder
2¾ teaspoons baking powder
½ teaspoon salt
1 teaspoon ground nutmeg
¼ teaspoon ground cardamom
½ cup (1 stick) plus 1 tablespoon unsalted butter,
    softened
Oil, for the bowl

Granulated sugar, for dusting doughnuts
Whole toasted pecans, for garnish

Special equipment:

Ice cream maker
Nonstick silicone baking mat or parchment paper
Standing mixer with dough hook
2-inch round biscuit cutter

To prepare the pecan bourbon ice cream: Add the cream, milk, and sugar to a large saucepan over medium heat. Bring just to a simmer. Remove from heat and add pecans. Blend with an immersion blender or transfer mixture to a blender and puree. Whisk in the egg yolks. Let the mixture steep in the refrigerator for 1 hour.

Strain the mixture through a fine-meshed sieve and discard the solids. Stir in the bourbon. Chill in the refrigerator for 2 hours or until cold. Freeze the mixture in an ice cream maker according to manufacturer's instructions.

To prepare the spice blend: Combine all ingredients in a small bowl with a whisk; set aside.

To prepare the squash cream: Add the kabocha or butternut squash puree, heavy cream, milk, 1 tablespoon prepared spice blend, and sugar to a medium saucepan over medium heat. Keep just below a simmer and whisk for 4 to 5 minutes, or until mixture is homogenous. Remove from the heat; puree the mixture with an immersion blender or transfer mixture to a blender and puree. Add the bloomed, drained gelatin sheet while the mixture is still hot, and whisk thoroughly. Strain mixture through a fine-meshed sieve and chill. Once chilled, and just before serving, whip mixture to soft peaks with an electric mixer.

To prepare the chocolate paint: Bring the water and sugar to a boil in a medium saucepan, whisking to make sure the sugar is dissolved. Remove from the heat and add the cocoa powder, whisking constantly. Return to the heat and bring back to a simmer, whisking constantly. Whisk and simmer for 1 minute, then remove from heat once more. Pour the mixture over the dark chocolate in a medium bowl and whisk until chocolate is melted and incorporated. Strain mixture through a fine-meshed sieve to remove any small lumps and refrigerate until chilled.

To prepare the pecan soil: Preheat oven to 350°F.

Add the pecans, brown sugar, flour, and salt to the bowl of a food processor and process until finely chopped. Transfer to bowl and drizzle with melted butter. Stir or mix by hand until the mixture looks sandy and mealy. Spread the mixture out on a baking sheet lined with a silicone baking mat or parchment paper. Bake for 10–12 minutes or until crumbly and dry.

To prepare the chocolate doughnuts: Combine all ingredients except butter in the bowl of a standing mixer and mix with dough hook on low speed just until the mixture comes together. Add the softened butter a piece at a time with the mixer running. Once butter is incorporated, mix on medium speed for 8 minutes.

Turn the dough out into an oiled bowl and cover; allow to rise for 30 minutes.

Punch the dough down and fold it over itself; allow to rise for 15 minutes more.

Place the dough in the refrigerator and chill for 30 minutes.

Once chilled, roll dough out on a floured surface to a ½-inch thickness and let sit for 10 minutes. Cut with a 2-inch round cutter and set aside until ready to serve.

To cook the doughnuts: Heat canola oil to 340°F in a deep saucepan or deep fryer. Drop in the doughnuts a few at a time and cook for about 2–3 minutes per side, until just browned. Drain on paper towels and immediately toss with granulated sugar.

To plate: Use a pastry brush to swipe chocolate paint in an arc on the plate. Sprinkle with pecan soil, then top with 3 chocolate doughnuts. Add a scoop of the pecan bourbon ice cream and a few dollops of the squash cream. Garnish with whole toasted pecans.

Banana Parfait with Cashew Ice Cream, Chocolate Soil & Rum Caramel

Pastry Chef Steven Cak's version of a banana parfait is elegant and refined. At Parkside, the parfait is frozen in silicone hemisphere molds (available at restaurant supply stores or online), though any shape would work well. It is garnished with passion fruit gel and cinnamon foam—Chef Cak recommends using fresh passion fruit and cinnamon-spiked whipped cream for garnishes at home. Recipe courtesy of Pastry Chef Steven Cak.

SERVES 2–3

For the banana parfait:

¾ cup mashed bananas
⅛ teaspoon cinnamon
½ cup plus 2 tablespoons mascarpone cheese
2 sheets gelatin, bloomed in cold water
2 egg whites
½ cup plus 2 tablespoons sugar
½ cup heavy cream

For the cashew ice cream:

2 cups heavy cream
2 cups whole milk
1¼ cups sugar
1¾ cups raw, unsalted cashews
12 egg yolks
2 tablespoons dark rum

For chocolate soil:

1¼ cup sugar
2 cups cashews
1¼ cups all-purpose flour
1¼ cups cocoa powder
2½ teaspoons salt
¾ cup (1½ sticks) unsalted butter, melted

For the chocolate paper:

½ cup (1 stick) plus 2 tablespoons unsalted butter, melted
¼ cup water
¾ cup sugar
¾ cup packed brown sugar
1 cup plus 1 tablespoon all-purpose flour
¼ cup cocoa powder

For the rum caramel:

2 cups heavy cream
1¾ cups sugar
1 tablespoon water
1 tablespoon rum (or more to taste)

Special equipment:

Ice cream maker
Nonstick silicone baking mat, parchment, or waxed paper
Hemisphere molds or other molds

To prepare the banana parfait: Whisk together the banana, cinnamon, and mascarpone in a large bowl.

Take one-fourth of the banana mixture and place in a separate heatproof bowl along with the bloomed, drained gelatin sheets. Place over a double boiler and whisk until gelatin is completely melted.

Pour the gelatin mixture into the remaining banana mixture and whisk together until homogenous. Set aside and let cool at room temperature.

Add the egg whites to the bowl of an electric mixer and whip on high. While whites are mixing, sprinkle sugar over them in several additions. Whip the whites and sugar to stiff peaks. Set aside.

Add the cream to the bowl of an electric mixer. Whip to soft peaks.

Add about one-third of the egg white mixture to the banana mixture and whisk vigorously to loosen it up. Fold in the remaining egg white mixture. Finally, lightly fold in the whipped cream.

Pipe the mixture into molds and freeze until solid.

To prepare the cashew ice cream: Add the cream, milk, and sugar to a large saucepan over medium heat. Bring just to a simmer. Remove from the heat and add cashews. Blend with an immersion blender or transfer mixture to a blender and puree. Whisk in the egg yolks. Let the mixture steep in the refrigerator for 1 hour.

Strain the mixture through a fine-meshed sieve and discard the solids. Stir in rum. Chill in the refrigerator for 2 hours or until cold. Freeze mixture in an ice cream maker according to manufacturer's instructions.

To prepare the chocolate soil: Combine the sugar, cashews, flour, cocoa powder, and salt to the bowl of a food processor and process until finely chopped. Transfer to a bowl and drizzle with melted butter. Stir or mix by hand until the mixture looks sandy and mealy. Spread the mixture out on a baking sheet lined with a silicone baking mat or parchment paper. Bake for 10–12 minutes or until crumbly and dry.

To prepare the chocolate paper: Preheat the oven to 350°F.

Whisk together butter and water in a small bowl. Set aside.

In a medium bowl, whisk together the sugar, brown sugar, flour, and cocoa powder. Drizzle with butter mixture and stir until a paste is formed. Spread mixture onto a baking sheet lined with a silicone baking mat or parchment paper in a thin layer. Bake until the chocolate paper stops bubbling, about 5–8 minutes. Remove from oven and let cool. Once cooled, break into shards.

To prepare the rum caramel: Add the cream to a medium saucepan over medium heat. Bring just to a simmer.

Meanwhile, add sugar and water to a separate medium saucepan over medium heat; do not stir. Allow the sugar to caramelize to a medium amber color. Remove from heat; carefully and gradually whisk in the hot cream (the mixture may spatter) and whisk together. Whisk in the rum and let sit for 30 minutes. Strain through a fine-meshed sieve.

To finish: Remove the parfaits from the freezer about 5 minutes before serving time. Make 4 piles of the chocolate soil on a plate (preferably rectangular). Top 3 of the piles with banana parfait hemispheres; top the fourth pile with a scoop of the cashew ice cream. Garnish with shards of chocolate paper and dollops of rum caramel.

The Steeping Room

11410 Century Oaks Terrace, Suite 112
Austin, TX 78758
(512) 977-8337
WWW.THESTEEPINGROOM.COM
Co-owners: Emily Morrison and Amy March

In the heart of the Domain residential and retail district in north Austin, The Steeping Room provides a peaceful respite. Locally owned by Amy March and Emily Morrison, this teahouse offers breakfast, lunch, dinner, and Sunday brunch in addition to a well-cultivated selection of organic and natural teas.

The interior of the restaurant is calming and Zen-like, with a clean and urban touch. As traditional teahouses often reflect the nature around them, the colors and textures at The Steeping Room reflect the natural aspects of Austin, and the simple, modern style is a nod to Austin's urban side. The result is a space that is welcoming, where guests can feel just as comfortable with a book and a cup of tea as with a group of friends or colleagues. March and Morrison wanted to create a community space with healthy, fresh food and the best teas available.

All of the food at The Steeping Room is made from scratch using local ingredients when possible. The cafe-style menu features food and pastries that are inspired by cultures that celebrate the tea experience, from Japan to the Mediterranean. A good place to start is with one of the tea services, which include sandwiches, spring rolls, or dolmas along with scones, brownies, or cookies and a pot of premium tea. Salads, soups, and sandwiches round out the lunch and dinner menus, while breakfast and brunch include chai-spiced french toast and organic oatmeal with banana brûlée. The food is fresh and healthy, and there are plenty of vegan, vegetarian, and gluten-free options.

Most importantly, there are so many wonderful teas available at The Steeping Room, and the staff is well trained to discuss, prepare, and serve them impeccably. Along with the popular flavored teas and blends, there are single-leaf teas from China, Taiwan, and Vietnam. The menu offers black, green, white, oolong, Pu-erh, and herbal teas, as well as one of the city's best cups of chai. Made fresh with cardamom, ginger, cinnamon, and clove, it's a far cry from the syrupy concoctions available at other places.

March and Morrison are excited about the recent opening of their second location in central Austin. With a similar design and menu, they hope to spread the community and culture of tea even more.

LEMON LAVENDER TEA CAKE

This beautiful cake is bright with lemon flavor, and the lavender adds a delicate herbal note. Be sure to make the icing rather thick, so it will drape nicely over the cake without dripping. Recipe courtesy of The Steeping Room.

SERVES 10–12

For the cake:

3 cups all-purpose flour
1 teaspoon baking soda
1½ teaspoons baking powder
¾ teaspoon salt
1 cup (2 sticks) unsalted butter, softened
1½ cups sugar
1 tablespoon lemon zest
1 tablespoon dried lavender flowers
4 eggs
½ teaspoon lemon extract
1 cup buttermilk

For the lemon glaze:

½ cup lemon juice
½ cup sugar
1 tablespoon plus 1 teaspoon honey

For the lemon lavender icing:

2 cups confectioners' sugar, plus more as needed
1 lemon
Water as needed

1 teaspoon dried lavender flowers, for garnish

To prepare the cake: Preheat the oven to 350°F. Butter and flour a 9-inch bundt pan.

Sift together the flour, baking soda, baking powder, and salt, and set aside.

In a separate bowl, beat the butter with an electric mixer until smooth. Add the sugar, lemon zest, and lavender, and beat until light and fluffy, 3–5 minutes. Add the eggs one at a time, beating well after each addition. Add the lemon extract and beat well.

On low speed, add the flour and buttermilk alternately in four equal additions.

Pour the batter into the prepared bundt pan and place on the center rack of the preheated oven. Bake until the cake pulls away from the edge of a pan and a toothpick comes out clean, about 50–60 minutes. Transfer to a cooling rack and allow the cake to cool in the pan completely. While the cake is baking, prepare the lemon glaze.

To prepare the lemon glaze: Combine all ingredients in a small stainless steel saucepan. Bring to a boil; reduce heat to low and simmer for 10–15 minutes until reduced by about one-third. Let cool.

When the cake is cooled, turn it out of the pan and brush with the lemon glaze.

To prepare the lemon lavender icing: Sift the confectioners' sugar into a medium bowl. With a fine grater, zest the skin of the whole lemon into the sugar. Squeeze the juice of the whole lemon through a sieve into the sugar. Stir to form a firm paste. Add water, 1 tablespoon at a time, until the icing is firm but can be very slowly poured over the top of the cake.

Pour the icing over the glazed cake, allowing it to drape slightly down the edges of the cake. Sprinkle lavender flowers over the top. The cake will keep, wrapped, at room temperature for up to 3 days.

Lenoir

1807 South 1st Street
Austin, TX 78704
(512) 215-9778
http://lenoirrestaurant.com/

Co-owners/Chefs: Todd Duplechan and Jessica Maher

In January of 2012, husband-and-wife team Todd Duplechan and Jessica Maher opened Lenoir, a tiny restaurant with limited seating and big ideas. Their goal was to create a neighborhood restaurant that was both sustainable and affordable, and from decor to food, they have accomplished it.

The entire restaurant was outfitted with repurposed materials, many from Duplechan's and Maher's own families. Designer Chris McCray was able to create an intimate, elegant space while maintaining the couple's goals of sustainability. The tables and stools were made from repurposed wood. The wine cabinet was once Duplechan's grandmother's armoire. The doilies that line the walls are family heirlooms, and the cast-iron pans in the kitchen once graced grandparents' kitchens. The result is a very personal space that is at once comforting and entirely unique.

Duplechan says that the style of Lenoir's menu is "hot weather food." He looks to other parts of the world with climates similar to Austin's and is inspired by the foods that are grown and served there. The food cultures of North Africa and Southeast Asia, south India and southern France all influence the ingredients and cooking style of Lenoir. Duplechan uses spice and acidity to brighten and highlight local produce and proteins. In keeping with his mission of sustainability, the chef cooks with wild, invasive species, bycatch, and produce from local farmers.

All of this results in an affordable three-course, thirty-five-dollar prix-fixe menu with dishes like crispy goat and potato terrine with harissa, fish curry with poha crust and heirloom tomatoes, and venison with wild ramps and fava bean ravioli. Maher creates desserts inspired by seasonal produce, such as a local strawberry pie with caramel rice flakes. Flavors of Texas mingle with those of Morocco and southern Spain, and Duplechan and Maher manage to bring them all together in a cohesive and exciting way.

Lenoir is a neighborhood bistro with good food at good prices, and guests can feel confident that their meal was honestly and sustainably sourced, prepared, and served.

Rosettas & Spicy Chocolate

Lenoir's rosette irons were a gift from Maher's grandmother. It seemed natural to offer these cookies and spiced chocolate for their winter menu. A nod to the classic Spanish churros and chocolate, the rosettas instantly became a guest favorite. Recipe courtesy of Chef Jessica Maher.

SERVES 4

For the spiced chocolate:

2¼ cups whole milk, divided
Finely grated zest of ½ orange
1 green cardamom pod
2 tablespoons sugar
1½ teaspoons cornstarch
⅛ teaspoon salt
8 ounces dark chocolate (at least 60%), chopped

For the rosettas:

1 whole egg, beaten
1½ teaspoon sugar
⅛ teaspoon salt
½ cup all-purpose flour
½ teaspoon orange zest, finely chopped
½ cup whole milk
Canola or grapeseed oil, for frying
Confectioners' sugar, for dusting

Special equipment:

Rosette irons

To prepare the spiced chocolate: Add 2 cups milk, orange zest, and cardamom to a medium saucepan over medium-high heat; bring to a boil.

In a small bowl, whisk together the sugar, cornstarch, and salt, then whisk in the remaining ¼ cup milk. Set aside.

When the milk reaches a boil, remove from heat and add the chocolate, stirring to melt. Return melted chocolate mixture to low heat and simmer for 30 minutes, whisking constantly. Add the cornstarch mixture and cook for another 10 minutes, whisking constantly. Chocolate should thickly coat a spoon. Strain through a fine-mesh sieve. Serve with rosettas (chocolate can be reheated slowly over low heat; add a bit more milk if it thickens too much).

To prepare the rosettas: Whisk the sugar and egg together until well combined. Add the salt, flour, and zest, then add the milk, and stir until the batter just comes together. Allow to rest for 15 minutes.

Heat the canola oil in a deep fryer or deep saucepan to 350°F, with the rosette irons resting in the oil. Pull out a rosette iron and allow the oil to drip off, then dip in the batter and drop back into the hot oil. Jiggle the mold a bit so the cookie will release, and continue cooking the rosette, flipping once, until golden. Use a slotted spoon to remove the rosette from the oil and drain on paper towels or a cooling rack. Repeat with remaining batter. Dust with confectioners' sugar and serve with a cup of the spiced chocolate.

Big Top Candy Shop

1706 South Congress Avenue
Austin, TX 78704
(512) 462-2220
www.facebook.com/bigtopcandyshop
Founder/Proprietor: Brandon Hodge

Austin's South Congress Avenue is chock-full of food carts, gift shops, restaurants, and costume stores. Perhaps the most whimsical and delicious of them all is Big Top Candy Shop, where founder and proprietor Brandon Hodge has created a sweet and funky wonderland of all things sweet.

With its checkerboard floor, striped walls, and circus memorabilia and decor, Big Top is a colorful, eccentric, and fanciful shop that makes people smile the moment they walk in. As if the atmosphere wasn't exciting enough, the shop is filled wall-to-wall with

candy. Bins of over forty flavors of saltwater taffy, a wall of jelly beans, and displays of old favorites like candy cigarettes and wax lips tempt children and adults alike. Rare finds like candy mushrooms and European chocolate bars sit alongside rock candy, lollipops, and Pixy Stix. The shop stays busy keeping Austin sugarcoated—it processes over a ton of candy per week.

To sweeten the deal, Texas-made chocolates, chocolate-covered bacon, truffles, and giant chocolate-covered marshmallows sit delicately in a display case, while the soda fountain churns out delights like perfect cherry limeades and refreshing cucumber sodas. Big Top takes pride in their real egg creams, made with classic Fox's U-Bet chocolate syrup. Also available are ice cream cones and floats, malts, and the popular Witch Doctor, a mix of Dr Pepper, tiger's blood syrup, and cream.

On any given day, there is a mixed bag of tourists and regulars browsing the shelves, waiting for a soda, or chatting with the friendly staff. It's difficult to leave the shop empty-handed—there is something at Big Top to entice everyone.

"King Killer" Bark

This concoction is an old favorite from Big Top's earliest days and has gained popularity over the years. In an effort to outdo their own chocolate-covered bacon, Big Top created this mix of Elvis's favorite combinations: peanut butter, bacon, jelly, and bananas. The result is a decadent and fantastical treat worthy of Big Top's sideshow atmosphere. Recipe courtesy of Brandon Hodge.

MAKES ABOUT 1½ POUNDS

3 cups semisweet chocolate chips
¼ teaspoon banana oil or extract (optional)
½ cup grape jelly
¾ cup smooth peanut butter
½ cup crumbled banana chips
½ cup bacon bits

Melt the chocolate chips in a large bowl in the microwave or over a double boiler, stirring until smooth. Stir in banana oil, if using.

Line a baking sheet with waxed paper, then spread the melted chocolate on the sheet in a layer ¼-inch thick. Spoon the grape jelly over the chocolate and swirl in the clumps with a knife to get even distribution throughout the chocolate.

Heat the peanut butter in a microwave for 10–15 seconds, just enough to reach a pourable consistency. Drizzle ½ cup of the peanut butter over the chocolate, swirling it in (save the remaining ¼ cup for later).

Sprinkle the banana chip crumbles over the bark, pressing them in slightly. Sprinkle the bacon bits on next, also pressing them into the chocolate slightly. Drizzle with the remaining peanut butter.

To set the bark, place the baking sheet in the freezer for about 20 minutes, until the chocolate becomes brittle. Do not freeze for more than about 30 minutes or the chocolate will start to speckle. Remove sheet from freezer and break apart into palm-size pieces.

Cucumber Soda

As Big Top faced its first summer, Brandon and his staff wanted to experiment with a light, refreshing drink to serve up at the soda fountain. After a lot of experimentation, they stumbled on just the right mix of crisp, fresh cucumber with a touch of sweetness. Recipe courtesy of Brandon Hodge.

MAKES 1 (20-OUNCE) SODA

1 whole cucumber
2 tablespoons simple syrup (page 24)
2 cups chilled seltzer water
Chipped ice, for serving
Juice of ½ lime (optional)

Special equipment:

Juicer

Juice the whole cucumber in a juicer, including peel (much of the flavor is in the peel). Strain the juice to remove any solid chunks.

Combine ¼ cup plus 2 tablespoons cucumber juice with the simple syrup, and chill until cold.

Pour cucumber syrup into a large glass and top with chilled seltzer water. Stir with three brisk stirs from the bottom up; avoid over stirring to keep the soda bubbly. Pour the cucumber soda over chipped ice in a serving glass. Squeeze in lime juice, if desired.

THE HIGHBALL

1142 SOUTH LAMAR BOULEVARD
AUSTIN, TX 78704
(512) 383-8309
WWW.THEHIGHBALL.COM
FOUNDER: TIM LEAGUE

The creative team behind Alamo Drafthouse (page 28) outdid themselves with The Highball. It is a restaurant, a cocktail bar, a bowling alley, a karaoke bar, a live music venue, and a dance party almost every night. There is so much to do and enjoy that one visit is never enough, and the top-quality food and cocktails keep guests coming back for more.

The centerpiece of The Highball is its fantastic bar, with new and classic cocktails created by the one of the city's most beloved barmen, Bill Norris. The oldfangled Aviation and Sazerac cocktails are just as tasty as the citrus-infused Witchy Woman. One side of the bar is outfitted with Skee-Ball machines and rent-by-the-hour bowling lanes, and upstairs, guests will find seven themed, private karaoke rooms. A stage and dance area toward the back offer an entertaining view to diners camped out in the comfortable booths near the front. On any given night, all of these areas are filled with locals enjoying the atmosphere and energy.

As if all of these amenities were not enough, The Highball also happens to serve excellent food. Dishes are creative and fun, highlighting the freshest local ingredients in a playful way. Smoked baby back ribs are glazed with a Dr Pepper sauce, and the Highball Hotwings are actually a fried quartered quail tossed with bacon fat and Sriracha. Gulf oysters are broiled with cilantro lime butter, and the gazpacho features smoked tomatoes and Texas olive oil. Entrees include fried (locally sourced) chicken, seared New York strip with a fried egg, and the popular Highball Burger topped with whiskey cheddar and caramelized onions. Desserts are just as tempting, from the dark, rich Chocolate Stout Cake to the tableside-prepared bourbon bread pudding jubilee and the decadent banana split.

The Highball is a cheeky, lively addition to Austin's South Lamar scene, and visitors can expect not only great entertainment but excellent food and cocktails as well.

CHOCOLATE STOUT CAKE

This rich chocolate cake with coffee liqueur–mascarpone filling and chocolate ganache icing will satisfy any chocolate lover's cravings. Served with fresh whipped cream and berries, it's a decadent dessert for a special occasion. Recipe courtesy of Executive Chef Trish Eichelberger.

SERVES 8–10

For the cake:

2 cups stout beer (such as Guinness)

1 pound (4 sticks) butter

1½ cups good-quality cocoa powder

4 cups all-purpose flour

4 cups sugar

1½ teaspoons salt

1 tablespoon baking soda

4 large eggs

1⅓ cups sour cream

For the filling:

2 cups mascarpone cheese

3 ounces coffee liqueur (such as Kahlúa)

For the frosting:

3½ cups chopped dark chocolate

Fresh berries or chocolate shavings, for garnish
  (optional)

To prepare the cake: Preheat the oven to 350°F. Butter and flour three 9-inch round cake pans.

Combine beer and butter in a large saucepan and bring to a simmer over medium heat. Whisk in cocoa powder until smooth. Remove from the heat and let cool slightly.

In a large bowl, whisk together flour, sugar, salt, and baking soda.

In a separate bowl, beat eggs and sour cream together with an electric mixer. Add stout-butter mixture and beat briefly until well combined. Gently fold in flour mixture with a rubber spatula.

Pour equal amounts of batter into each cake pan. Bake about 35 minutes, or until a toothpick inserted in the center of each cake comes out clean. Cool on a baking rack.

Remove cakes from pans and trim any mounded cake tops to create three flat pieces.

To prepare the filling: Combine the mascarpone and coffee liqueur in a medium bowl; whisk together until well blended. Do not overmix or the cheese will curdle.

To prepare the frosting: Heat the dark chocolate slowly in a double boiler until melted.

To assemble: Place one cake round on a serving platter or cake stand. Top with half of the filling. Top with second cake round and the rest of the filling; finish with the last cake round. Frost the entire cake with the melted dark chocolate. Any imperfections can easily be covered with fresh berries.

Uchi

801 South Lamar Boulevard
Austin, TX 78704
(512) 916-4808
www.uchiaustin.com/uchi
Owner/Executive Chef: Tyson Cole; Director of Culinary
Operations/Pastry Chef: Philip Speer

As one of Austin's first high-end, modern restaurants, Uchi has been groundbreaking for Austin's food scene. When Uchi opened in 2003, it didn't cater to the existing Austin market—it challenged restaurantgoers to taste and accept a new type of food experience.

Uchi means "house" in Japanese, and the restaurant is a beautifully updated house with a small front patio and cozy indoor seating. Only a limited number of reservations are available each night, but diners are willing to wait an hour or more for an available table or seat at the sushi bar. Not just a sushi restaurant, Uchi serves inspired and beautifully presented plates of the freshest ingredients available.

Owner, executive chef, and recipient of the 2011 Best Chef Southwest Award from the James Beard Foundation, Tyson Cole spent over a decade studying and honing his sushi skills and techniques. At Uchi, he uses those skills to create foods that are based on Japanese techniques and ingredients, with playful updates and innovative twists. Fresh nigiri and sashimi are served alongside Uchiviche, a stunning presentation of raw salmon and striped bass, tomato, bell pepper, garlic, and cilantro. Oak-grilled escolar and baby octopus share the table with soft-shell crab rolls and pork jowl with brussels sprout kimchee. For the less adventurous, the Bacon Steakie (pork belly, citrus, and Thai basil) and the Shag Roll (tempura-fried salmon, avocado, and sun-dried tomato) are approachable and delicious. Executive Pastry Chef Philip Speer's desserts are fantastical creations with subtle flavors and elegant presentations. The peanut butter semifreddo is an artfully composed plate with golden raisin puree, apple-miso sorbet, ground peanut brittle, and dehydrated apple. Delicate and yet assertive, the desserts at Uchi are not to be missed.

Diners can sit at the sushi bar and snack on nigiri and sake, or dive in for a multicourse meal that may last an entire evening. For a special occasion, ask for the *omakase* menu, for which the chef chooses ten or more courses based on what is freshest and most inspiring at the moment. Waitstaff are highly trained to guide diners through the meal, explaining dishes, suggesting menu items, and answering any questions with full and knowledgeable responses. While the food and service are excellent, the Uchi experience as a whole is unparalleled.

Even as new restaurants pop up around the city, Uchi still serves one of the most sought-after meals in Austin. It continues to innovate and break new ground, to surprise diners, and to entice guests to taste and experience something creative and new.

Coffee Panna Cotta with Mango Yolk

Pastry Chef Philip Speer's creation is fun and surprising—once the panna cotta is broken open with a spoon, the bright yellow "mango yolk" oozes out. The photograph features white chocolate "paper" and white chocolate "soil," which are not included in the recipe due to multiple specialty ingredients and techniques. Instead, Chef Speer has provided a recipe for mango paper, which is easier for the home cook. Be sure to start this recipe at least a day in advance. Recipe courtesy of Pastry Chef Philip Speer.

SERVES 6

For the coffee milk:

½ cup whole milk
⅓ cup whole coffee beans

For the mango paper:

½ cup mango puree (available in specialty markets,
    or use frozen mangos pureed in a food processor)
4 tablespoons sugar
1 extra-large egg white

For the mango yolk:

¾ cup plus 2 tablespoons mango puree
¼ cup water
4 tablespoons plus 1½ teaspoons sugar

For the white chocolate sorbet:

1½ cups water
1 cup plus 6 tablespoons plus 1 teaspoon sugar
½ teaspoon salt
3 ounces white chocolate

For the coffee soil:

6 tablespoons sugar
1 cup macadamia nuts
4 tablespoons cocoa powder
1 teaspoon salt
6 tablespoons flour
¼ cup ground coffee beans
7 tablespoons melted unsalted butter

For the coffee panna cotta:

½ teaspoon salt
6 tablespoons teaspoons sugar
2 sheets gelatin, bloomed in cold water for 3–4 minutes
1 cup heavy whipping cream

Special equipment:

6 (3-ounce) silicone hemisphere molds, available in
    restaurant supply stores or online
Ice cream maker

To prepare the coffee milk: Bring the milk and coffee beans to a boil in a small saucepan over high heat. Remove from heat and let steep overnight. The next day, strain out the beans and refrigerate the coffee milk.

To prepare the mango paper: Preheat the oven to 100°F. Combine all the ingredients in a bowl; using a hand mixer, blend until well combined. Spread the mixture thinly on a baking sheet and place in the low-heated oven overnight to dry and crisp. The next day, break into shards.

To prepare the mango yolk: Bring all the ingredients to a boil over high heat. Remove from heat and cool slightly. Pour into small (½-ounce) hemisphere molds (available online or in specialty cookware stores; other shapes are fine as long as they are smaller than the panna cotta molds) and freeze overnight.

To prepare the white chocolate sorbet: Bring the water, sugar, and salt to a boil in a medium saucepan. Remove from heat and add white chocolate. Using a hand mixer, blend until well combined; let cool. Once cooled, churn mixture in an ice cream maker according to manufacturer's directions. Freeze until ready to use.

To prepare the coffee soil: Preheat the oven to 350°F. In a food processor, combine all ingredients except butter; process until it reaches a fine crumb. Pour the crumbs into a mixing bowl and add butter; mix gently by hand until well combined (mixture will be crumbly, with some sandy and some larger crumb textures). Spread the crumb mixture onto a large baking sheet lined with parchment paper, and bake 10–12 minutes; let cool. Once cooled, crush the soil and store in an airtight container until ready to use.

To prepare the coffee panna cotta: Bring ¼ cup plus 2 tablespoons of the prepared coffee milk (save the rest for another use), salt, and sugar to a boil in a medium saucepan. Remove from heat; add bloomed gelatin. Using a hand mixer, blend until well combined. Let cool to room temperature.

In a separate bowl, whip heavy cream into soft peaks. Quickly whisk the coffee mixture into the whipped cream. Divide mixture into six (3-ounce) hemisphere molds. Top each mold with a frozen mango yolk (curved side down), and push into the center of the cream mixture; the yolks must be thoroughly covered and centered in the mixture to avoid them leaking or being seen through the panna cotta. Place the filled molds in the freezer for about 3 hours, or until set.

When the panna cottas are frozen solid, remove from the molds and place them flat side down on a baking sheet lined with parchment paper. Refrigerate about 4 hours, or until thawed.

To serve: Cover half of a plate (preferably round) with coffee soil. Place coffee panna cotta next to the soil. Place a scoop of white chocolate sorbet onto the mound of coffee soil, and finish by standing 2 shards of mango paper in the coffee soil.

Peanut Butter Semifreddo
with Apple Miso Sorbet

This beautiful dessert features several interesting flavors and textures that come together for an elegant dish. Uchi makes their own peanut brittle and dehydrated apples, but they can easily be replaced by store-bought versions. Recipe courtesy of Pastry Chef Philip Speer.

SERVES 8

For the semifreddo:

1½ cups cold heavy cream
¼ teaspoon salt
2¼ teaspoons vanilla extract
½ cup (4 ounces) cream cheese, at room temperature
½ cup creamy peanut butter
½ cup plus 1 tablespoon sugar

For the golden raisin puree:

2 cups golden raisins
½ cup water
½ cup sake
½ cup mirin
½ teaspoon salt

For the apple miso sorbet:

2 cups roughly chopped, unpeeled Fuji apple
¼ cup miso paste
2 cups simple syrup (page 24)
½ cup water
1 teaspoon salt
Ground peanut brittle, for garnish
Dehydrated apple slices, for garnish

Special equipment:

Ice cream maker
Squeeze bottle

To prepare the peanut butter semifreddo: Combine the heavy cream, salt, and vanilla in the bowl of an electric mixer. Whip to soft peaks; keep in refrigerator.

In a separate bowl, combine cream cheese, peanut butter, and sugar. Using an electric mixer, beat well until mixture is smooth. Add half the refrigerated whipped cream, and beat until well mixed.

With a spatula, gently fold in the remaining whipped cream. Pour mixture into a rectangular terrine mold (or desired smaller molds) lined with plastic wrap. Cover tightly and freeze for at least 4 hours.

To prepare the golden raisin puree: Combine all ingredients in a small saucepan. Bring to a boil; remove from heat. Let raisins sit in the saucepan for 30 minutes to rehydrate them.

Pour cooled raisin mixture into a blender and puree until smooth. Refrigerate in a squeeze bottle until serving.

Start assembly 30 minutes before serving time. Remove terrine from freezer. With a hot knife, slice into ¾-inch thick slices. Place each slice on a plate and refrigerate until the center is partially frozen and the outside is creamy and soft, about 30 minutes.

To prepare the apple miso sorbet: Combine apples and miso paste in a blender and puree until well combined. Add simple syrup, water, and salt, and puree until smooth. Chill mixture thoroughly, then freeze in an ice cream machine according to manufacturer's instructions.

To serve: Add a scoop of the apple miso sorbet on one end of the semifreddo slice and drizzle with the golden raisin puree. Garnish with ground peanut brittle and dehydrated apple slices.

ASTI TRATTORIA

408C EAST 43RD STREET
AUSTIN, TX 78751
(512) 451-1218
WWW.ASTIAUSTIN.COM
OWNERS: EMMETT AND LISA FOX

In the heart Austin's Hyde Park neighborhood sits a quaint center of activity, anchored by a few restaurants, a grocery store, bakeries, and the like. One of the cornerstones of the lot is ASTI Trattoria, which serves inspired Italian food.

Owners Emmett and Lisa Fox met in Boston, where Emmett discovered his love for Italian cuisine and Lisa fine-tuned her pastry skills. They moved to Austin and stepped into the restaurant scene, cooking and baking at several top eateries before opening ASTI in 2000. The restaurant is a perfect mix of Emmett's passion for the Italian style of cooking and Lisa's love of modern style and great pastries.

The dining room is lined with windows and cozy tables perfect for romantic evenings. Guests can also choose to sit at the counter, where they can have a prime view of the chefs crafting each dish. A wall of expertly chosen Italian wines provides an elegant backdrop, and the clean and modern aesthetic feels both upscale and relaxed.

The menu highlights the best of Italy as well as the best ingredients available. Antipasti include house-made bread sticks and grilled octopus, and the seasonal soups are not to be missed. Local farm eggs grace the spaghetti carbonara and a salad of radicchio, frisée, and fontina. Crispy pizza crusts are topped with house-made sausage, and pan-seared cod is paired with littleneck clams and fennel. At lunchtime, pizzas, panini, and pasta are available, as well as flavorful risotto and filling salads. Comforting bowls of creamy polenta come topped with grilled eggplant or grilled sausage.

Lisa's desserts are classic versions of Italian favorites, with an eye on quality ingredients and balanced flavors. The *affogato,* a bowl of vanilla bean gelato topped with hot espresso, comes with fluffy fried beignets, while the airy Ricotta Brûlée (page 198) is topped with brandied cherries. ASTI continuously edits and updates its menu with the seasons, and locals visit year-round for a refined, intimate meal.

Classic Tiramisu

Lisa was happy to share her version of this classic Italian dessert. At ASTI, the dessert is frozen in a terrine mold to create beautiful layered slices, but home cooks can use individual ramekins or a baking dish to assemble the dessert. Freezing the tiramisu makes it easier to slice, but it would be fine to serve the dessert after a short refrigeration. Recipe courtesy of Lisa Fox.

SERVES 8–10

12 ounces mascarpone

7 egg yolks

½ cup plus 2 tablespoons sugar

6 tablespoons Marsala

1 cup heavy cream

24 ladyfingers

1 cup espresso

½ cup shaved chocolate (optional)

Spread out the mascarpone in a large bowl and let it come to room temperature.

In a separate stainless steel bowl, whisk yolks, sugar, and Marsala together. Place bowl over a saucepan filled with 2–4 inches of simmering water; do not let the water touch the bottom of the bowl. Whisk the egg mixture over simmering water until yolks begin to cook and mixture thickens to create a zabaglione, about 10 minutes. Remove from heat and pour zabaglione into a cool bowl. Whip with an electric mixer on medium speed about 10 minutes, until cooled to room temperature.

Add the cooled zabaglione to the mascarpone and mix together until smooth.

In a separate bowl, whip heavy cream to medium stiff peaks. Gently fold the whipped cream into the mascarpone mixture. Refrigerate until ready to use.

Heavily brush both sides of each ladyfinger with espresso. Let rest about 10 minutes; break one open to check that the espresso has soaked the outer edges at least halfway through. If it hasn't, brush with a bit more espresso.

Line the inside of a terrine mold, baking dish, or ramekins with plastic wrap. Cover the bottom of the terrine with a layer of soaked ladyfingers. Layer in half of the cream mixture. Sprinkle with ¼ cup shaved chocolate, if desired. Repeat layers of ladyfingers, cream mixture, and chocolate shavings. Top with the remaining ladyfingers. Cover with plastic wrap and freeze for at least 6 hours.

Unmold and cut into slices (the terrine is easiest to cut when it is frozen). Refrigerate slices for 2 hours to thaw before serving.

RICOTTA BRÛLÉE

These individual desserts are fun to create and to serve. You'll need a kitchen torch to caramelize the sugar on top, and the number of servings depends on the size of your ramekins. Lisa recommends serving these with fresh cherries or figs. Recipe courtesy of Lisa Fox.

SERVES 6–8

12 ounces cream cheese, at room temperature
1 cup whole milk ricotta
1 teaspoon vanilla extract or ½ vanilla bean
1 cup sugar, plus more for caramelizing on top
2 eggs
2 egg whites
1 cup heavy cream

Special equipment:

Kitchen torch

In a large bowl, beat the cream cheese with an electric mixer until smooth. Add ricotta, vanilla (or scraped vanilla bean), and 1 cup sugar, and continue to beat. Add eggs and egg whites one at a time, beating after each addition. Add cream and beat well. This mixture can be made up to 2 days in advance.

Preheat the oven to 250°F.

Scoop the cream mixture into individual ramekins. Place ramekins in a baking dish and fill with water to halfway up the sides of the ramekins. Bake for 30–40 minutes. The brûlée will set up in the middle but just barely start to turn golden brown around the edges. Remove from the water bath and let come to room temperature. Refrigerate at least 4 hours before serving.

Sprinkle each ramekin with an even coat of granulated sugar. Using a kitchen torch, melt the sugar until it turns a lovely dark brown.

POLKADOTS CUPCAKE FACTORY

2826 RIO GRANDE STREET, SUITE B
AUSTIN, TX 78705
(512) 476-3687
WWW.POLKADOTSCUPCAKEFACTORY.COM
OWNERS: BEN AND OLGA LEE

In the summer of 2008, Ben and Olga Lee opened Polkadots Cupcake Factory in a tiny house that was built in 1908. Olga had earned a bachelor's degree in chemical engineering, with hopes of working in food chemistry and production. She planned on getting her master's degree, but an ad for a California culinary school grabbed her attention, and she realized that her heart was set on the creative pursuit of the culinary arts.

After graduating from the California School of Culinary Arts, Olga returned with Ben to Austin and started making plans for the bake shop. She spent her time testing recipes at home while Ben roamed the streets of Austin looking for the perfect location.

They outfitted their new space with pink tables, display cases, and espresso machines. Polkadots is now one of the city's favorite bakeries with its quaint interior, daily rotating cupcake specials, and beautiful cookies and cakes.

The bake shop is perhaps best known for its excellent cupcakes, which can be purchased in-store or ordered in large quantities in advance. Basic flavors like vanilla, triple chocolate, and red velvet are displayed alongside strawberry-coconut, cookies and cream, and Fluffernutter. Aside from these tasty treats, Polkadots creates whimsical custom cakes for special occasions, with a myriad of flavors like honey and chai, Italian cream, and banana Nutella. Cleverly decorated cookies are perfect for parties and gifts, and all are created to not only look beautiful, but taste delicious as well.

The charming tables and decor inside and on the front patio make Polkadots the perfect spot for an afternoon treat of coffee and a black bottom cupcake.

PUMPKIN CUPCAKES WITH CREAM CHEESE ICING

Polkadots offers seasonal cupcakes like this pumpkin cupcake that is available in the fall and winter. At the bakery, the icing is piped on top in a lovely swirl. Recipe courtesy of Chef Olga Lee.

MAKES 10 CUPCAKES.

For the cupcakes:

½ cup plus ⅓ cup granulated sugar

1 cup all-purpose flour, sifted

1 teaspoon baking powder

½ teaspoon baking soda

½ teaspoon salt

1 teaspoon cinnamon

7½ ounces (about 1 cup minus 2 tablespoons) pumpkin puree

2 eggs, at room temperature

½ cup vegetable oil

For the cream cheese icing:

1 cup (2 sticks) European-style unsalted butter (like Plugrá), at room temperature

2 cups confectioners' sugar

8 ounces cream cheese, at room temperature

¾ teaspoon vanilla bean paste or vanilla extract

To prepare the cupcakes: Preheat the oven to 350°F. Line a cupcake/muffin tin with 10 paper liners (leave two muffin cups empty).

Mix all dry cupcake ingredients in a bowl and set aside.

Place pumpkin puree in a large mixing bowl. Add eggs, one at a time, beating with a mixer at low speed after each addition until smooth. Add dry ingredients and oil alternately to pumpkin mixture, beating at medium speed after each addition until smooth.

Using an ice cream scoop to make uniform-size cupcakes, scoop batter into the 10 paper liners. Bake for 18–20 minutes, or until toothpick inserted in center comes out clean. Let cool on a rack.

To prepare the cream cheese icing: Combine the butter and confectioners' sugar in a large mixing bowl. With a mixer, beat until light and fluffy and doubled in size. Add cream cheese and vanilla slowly, beating until smooth.

Frost the cupcakes with the cream cheese icing.

LA PATISSERIE

602 West Annie Street
Austin, TX 78704
(512) 912-0033
http://lpaustin.com/
Owner/Baker: Soraiya Nagree

It had long been a dream of Soraiya Nagree's to bake French pastries in her own little shop. With the opening of La Patisserie, that dream came true. Starting in 2006, Nagree delivered *macarons* and other pastries under the name Luxe Sweets; now those pastries sit in a glass display case in her own bakery.

La Patisserie is located in a cozy renovated house on a quiet side street in south Austin. Inside, the main dining room is light and airy, with armchairs and cafe tables. A side room is outfitted with a play area stocked with toys as well as a few rocking chairs.

Moms are grateful for this chance to enjoy coffee and pastries and chat with friends as their children keep occupied within sight. Not many cafes offer something like this to parents, but Nagree knew, as a new mom herself, that it would be appreciated.

The display case is filled with beautiful croissants, cinnamon buns, palmiers, éclairs, and madeleines. Trays of delicate French *macarons* with flavors like cardamom-honey-orange and milk chocolate–Earl Grey are tempting, as are Nagree's decadent cakes. Her specialty is the chocolate-raspberry-pistachio cake, a creation that is based on three of her favorite flavors. Cakes are available whole or by the slice. During lunchtime, La Patisserie also serves salads, sandwiches, soups, and tarts that feature seasonal produce, and espresso drinks and tea are always available.

While the bakery does steady business serving walk-in customers looking for a pastry and coffee, Nagree still offers many of the specialty orders that Luxe Sweets provided. Biscotti, fudge, cookies, brownies, and *macarons* can be locally delivered or shipped anywhere in the United States. For regulars, however, the best way to enjoy Nagree's pastries is from a cozy armchair at La Patisserie.

Gâteau de Pistache, Framboise, et Chocolat
PISTACHIO, RASPBERRY & CHOCOLATE CAKE

Chef Nagree came up with this beautiful cake recipe while pondering her three favorite flavors: pistachio, chocolate, and raspberry. A slice of this cake is colorful and decadent, making it a great option for a special birthday or celebratory dessert. Recipe courtesy of Chef Soraiya Nagree.

SERVES 8–10

For the chocolate cake:

1¾ cups cake flour
¾ cup unsweetened cocoa powder
1¼ teaspoons baking soda
¾ teaspoon salt
½ teaspoon baking powder
2 cups sugar
12 tablespoons (1½ sticks) unsalted butter, softened
3 eggs
4 teaspoons vanilla extract
1½ cups buttermilk

For the pistachio paste:

1¾ cups ground pistachios
2¹/₃ cups confectioners' sugar
1 cup (8 ounces) unsalted butter, softened

For the chocolate ganache:

8 ounces high-quality bittersweet or dark
  chocolate, chopped
1 cup heavy cream
½ cup (4 ounces) unsalted butter, cut into pieces
  and softened

¼ cup melted raspberry jam (heated in microwave),
plus ½ cup raspberry jam
Fresh raspberries, ground pistachios, chocolate batons,
for garnish (optional)

Special equipment:

Standing mixer with whisk attachment

To prepare the cake: Preheat oven to 350°F.
Butter and flour three 9-inch diameter round
baking pans. Line the bottom of each pan with a
circle of parchment paper.

Sift the cake flour, cocoa powder, baking soda,
salt, and baking powder into a medium bowl. Set
aside.

Combine sugar and butter and beat with an
electric mixer until well blended. Add eggs one
at a time, beating well after each addition. Add
vanilla and beat well.

Add the sifted dry ingredients alternately with the
buttermilk, beating well between each addition.

Divide the batter equally among the three
prepared pans.

Bake about 25–30 minutes, or until a cake tester
or toothpick inserted in the center of each
cake comes out with some moist crumbs still
attached.

Cool cakes in the pans for about 15 minutes. Turn
out onto racks and peel off parchment paper;
cool completely.

To prepare the pistachio paste: Combine
all ingredients in a mixer fitted with a whisk
attachment. Whisk until pale green and creamy.

To prepare the chocolate ganache: Place
chocolate in a mixing bowl and make a well in
the center. Bring heavy cream just to a boil in a
small saucepan; pour hot cream into the center
of the chocolate well. Let the bowl sit for about
5 minutes. Stir to melt chocolate. Once the
chocolate is melted, stir in the butter, piece by
piece, until smooth and incorporated.

To assemble the cake: Level each cake round so
that they are flat across the top. Place one cake
on a cake stand. Brush the top with the melted
raspberry jam.

Spread the pistachio paste evenly across the
cake, leaving an empty ¼-inch border around the
edge to allow for spreading.

Top with another cake layer. Spread the
nonmelted raspberry jam across the top of this
layer, again leaving an empty ¼-inch border
around the edge to allow for spreading.

Top with the last cake layer. Coat the entire cake
with a layer of chocolate ganache. Refrigerate
about 30 minutes until the ganache has set. Coat
with another layer of ganache. Decorate the top
with fresh raspberries, pistachio powder, and
chocolate batons, as desired.

Recipe Index

General Index

About the Author

Crystal Esquivel is an author and registered dietitian who has been an Austin-area foodie for the last ten years. She maintains a blog, *Poco-Cocoa*, in which she chronicles her cooking adventures in her own kitchen and her eating adventures in Austin's numerous restaurants. She is the author of the *Food Lovers' Guide to Austin* (Globe Pequot Press).

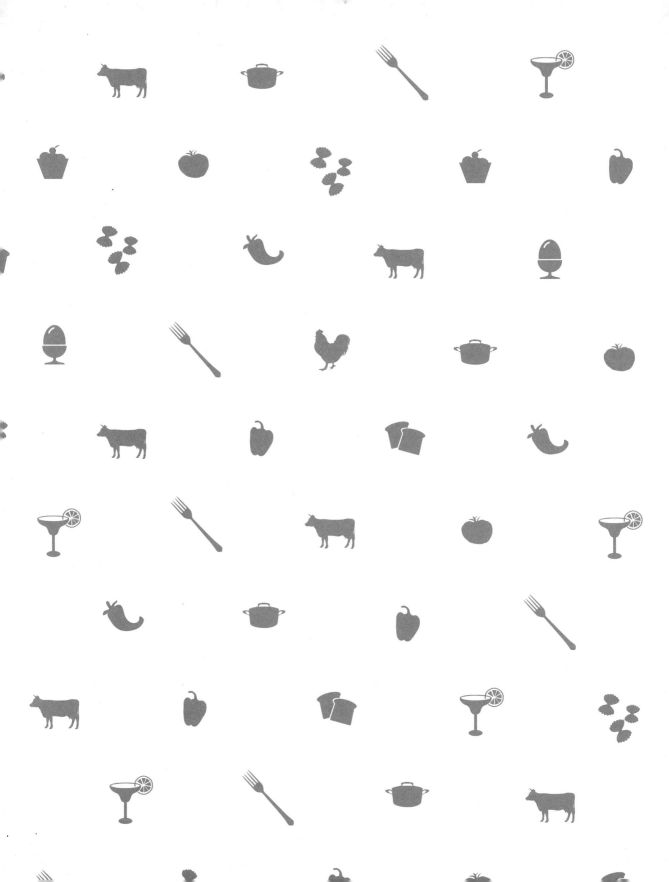